DATE DUE

SEP 24 2004			
OCT 05 2004			

Lifesaving Letters

8579

This document of identity is issued with the approval of His Majesty's Government in the United Kingdom to young persons to be admitted to the United Kingdom for educational purposes under the care of the Inter-Aid Committee for children.

THIS DOCUMENT REQUIRES NO VISA.

PERSONAL PARTICULARS.

Name ROTH MILENA

Sex FEMALE Date of Birth 3.10.32.

Place PRAG

Full Names and Address of Parents

ROTH, Emil a Anna

22, Simackova

PRAG

Lifesaving Letters

A CHILD'S FLIGHT FROM THE HOLOCAUST

MILENA ROTH

Foreword by David Patterson

A Samuel and Althea Stroum Book

UNIVERSITY OF WASHINGTON PRESS

Seattle and London

This book is published with the assistance of a grant
from the Stroum Book Fund, established through the generosity
of Samuel and Althea Stroum.

Printed in the United States of America
Designed by Pamela Canell
08 07 06 05 04 5 4 3 2 1

University of Washington Press
P.O. Box 50096
Seattle, WA 98145-5096
www.washington.edu/uwpress

Library of Congress Cataloging-in-Publication Data
available from the Library of Congress
ISBN 0-295-98377-9

The paper used in this publication is acid-free and recycled from 10 percent post-consumer and at least 50 percent pre-consumer waste. It meets the minimum requirements of American National Standard for Information Sciences—Permanence of Paper for Printed Library Materials, ANSI Z39.48–1984. ♾ ♲

The hymn "All Things Bright and Beautiful," quoted in chapter 4,
was written by Cecil Frances Alexander in 1848.

IN LOVING MEMORY OF MY PARENTS

Anna Rothová

24 November 1905–8 March 1944

Emil Roth

10 November 1902–8 March 1944

CONTENTS

FOREWORD

Lifesaving Letters: Contexts and Implications

Spanning the years of 1930 through 1942, the lifesaving letters in this volume were written during Europe's descent into a long night of death. They were written over a time when the continent was transformed from a relatively civilized world into the anti-world known as the concentrationary universe. Written by a mother who saved her daughter, these letters rise up from the depths of that universe and call out to a land where Jewish children were not hunted down and murdered. Yes, *Jewish children were hunted down and murdered:* that is a defining feature of the Nazis and the chief context for these lifesaving letters.

By September 1930, when Anna Roth wrote the first of these letters, the Nazi Party had been in existence for more than ten years. In the course of those ten years they had become experts in propaganda. During that time their propaganda campaigns focused on Germany's widespread unemployment and its loss of respect among the nations. But anti-Semitism was always the basis of their thinking: Jews were to blame for Germany's economic collapse and humiliation. Indeed, the chief cause of all of Germany's problems, the Nazis maintained, was "International World Jewry." The Jews, said the Nazis, controlled the Western "plutocracies" and the Russian Bolsheviks. They preyed upon German women and poisoned German blood. The inventors of humanism, liberalism, conscience, and compassion, they threatened the fabric of human civilization. In short, the Jews were not just a political, economic, or moral danger. No, they were a cosmic, satanic evil that threatened the very soul of humanity.

These ideas won for the Nazis just over one-third of the seats in the Reichstag in the elections of November 1932. By January 30, 1933, Adolf Hitler was chancellor of Germany, and by July 14, 1933, the National Socialist Party was the only political party in Germany that still had legal status. That same month the new Nazi Reich received its first diplomatic recognition—from the Vatican. All of this unfolded in a democracy in the heart of Christendom. But it did not come out of nowhere.

From the early days of the new religion, there arose in Christianity what its leaders referred to as "the teaching of contempt" for the Jews. Saint Cyprian (d. 258), for example, declared that "the peoplehood of the Jews has been cancelled."[1] Similarly, from Saint Augustine (354–430) to Martin Luther (1483–1546), Christian thinkers insisted that Jews should be kept in misery to serve as an example of those who reject the salvation of Christ. Added to centuries of Christian hatred for the Jews was the philosophical contempt for Judaism spawned by the Enlightenment. Immanuel Kant (1724–1804), for example, insisted that "the euthanasia of Judaism is the pure moral religion,"[2] and Hegel (1770–1831) blamed the Jews for refusing to "die as Jews."[3] As philosophy continued to develop, it did no better than Christianity had done with regard to the "Jewish Question." To be sure, the Nazis came to power just as philosophy reached its height in Martin Heidegger (1889–1976), who in 1933 extolled the "magnificence and greatness" of Nazism—a position he never recanted.[4]

Milena Roth was barely a year old when Heidegger was making such statements. As Milena grew, so did the project to murder her and her people. On September 15, 1935, the Nazis passed the Nuremberg Laws, which, according to various classes of "mixed bloods," defined a Jew as anyone who had a Jewish grandparent. The Nuremberg Laws, moreover, make it clear that the Nazis' hatred for the Jews was not just a matter of race, since the Jewish grandparent was anyone who attended a synagogue; converts to Judaism were also defined as Jews under the new Nazi law. For the Nazis, race was a *metaphysical category,* and not just a biological classification. Hence, said Nazi philosopher Alfred Rosenberg (1893–1946), "our race has been poisoned by *Judaism,*"[5] and not merely by Jewish blood.

By the time Milena turned five, on October 3, 1937, the Jews had turned over their property to the Reich. A year later, on October 1, 1938, the Nazis annexed the Sudetenland, a region that was very close to the Roths' hometown of Prague: they knew the Nazi beast was closing in on its Jewish prey. When the Nazis entered Czechoslovakia, on March 15, 1939, Anna Roth and thousands of other Jewish mothers must have known that their children were somehow marked for death. For it is clear that they knew they had to get their children out of Europe.

THE KINDERTRANSPORT

The realization that Jewish lives were in danger was driven home in the aftermath of *Kristallnacht,* when on November 9, 1938, a wave of unprecedented violence against the Jews swept through Germany. Much to their credit, when the British received news of that horror, they responded by forming the World Movement for the Care of Children from Germany. The World Movement served as an umbrella organization for a number of other groups, including the Jewish Refugees Committee, the Quakers, and various churches. There were also many individuals who worked through the movement.

On November 21, 1938, the British government announced its decision to allow an unspecified number of children up to age seventeen from German-occupied lands to enter the United Kingdom as "transmigrants." It was estimated that the cost of bringing a single child to British shores was fifty pounds. On December 8, former prime minister Stanley Earl Baldwin delivered a passionate radio address in which he appealed to the British citizens to post the necessary fifty-pound bond. Within a short time, 500,000 pounds had been raised, making it possible to transport 10,000 children to the British Isles. News of the Kindertransport spread rapidly, and before long thousands of parents were clambering to get their children on a transport. Of the 9,354 children who escaped the Nazis between December 1938 and September 1939, 70 percent were Jewish.

In March 1939 the World Movement for the Care of Children from Germany merged with the Children's Inter-Aid Committee to form the

Refugee Children's Movement (RCM). Local auxiliary committees took on the task of finding homes for the children and arranging for their education. In Europe the children's emigration departments of the central Jewish organizations in Germany, Austria, and Czechoslovakia made the difficult decisions regarding who would go and who would stay. In addition to the children designated for the Kindertransport, they managed to get 500 youngsters into Great Britain as members of Youth Aliya groups, as well as another 1,350 who were to be part of "agricultural training" programs for British-ruled Palestine.

The children of the Kindertransport were divided into two categories: those who had private sponsors and those who were sponsored by the RCM. Upon their arrival in Britain they were placed in reception facilities and then sent to their new foster homes. The matter of placing Jewish children in non-Jewish homes was extremely controversial at the time, but it was soon clear that it simply could not be avoided. While it was true that there were 350,000 Jews living in Britain at the time, the vast majority of them lived on extremely modest incomes and could not afford the fifty-pound bond. With Jewish children being placed in Christian homes, the Chief Rabbi's Religious Emergency Council issued several pleas to host families that they should not attempt to convert Jewish children to Christianity. Almost all the Jewish children placed with Christian families, however, grew up without any Jewish learning or any real sense of their Jewish identity.

To the extent that they could find the means, British Jews responded generously to the appeals for funds to bring Jewish children to the British Isles. But they also felt a certain apprehension that such an influx of new Jewish refugees would further aggravate the anti-Semitism that was already quite pronounced in British society. Professional organizations, certain segments of the press, and the resurgent British fascist movement were extremely vocal in their opposition to the "refuJews," so that the Jewish concern was understandable. The government issued leaflets apologizing to the public for the influx of refugees. The newly arrived children were themselves given instructions not to speak German in public, to avoid complaining, to assert their loyalty to their new land at every opportunity, and never to make any comparisons between Britain and Germany. Thus, having made their way to Britain, the Jewish children did not exactly arrive at their new "home." Rather, they had managed to exchange one hiding place for another—one much more secure, to be sure, but a hiding place nevertheless.

By the end of August 1939 the BCM had run out of money and imposed a freeze on the acceptance of any more children. Milena, then, was fortunate to get out when she did, on July 18, 1939. On that day, mother and daughter parted as the little girl boarded a train for a strange land. And so at the age of six Milena became a "refuJew." By the time she turned seven, the following October, the Nazis had conquered Poland, and the Final Solution to the Jewish Question was under way.

THE FINAL SOLUTION

While Milena was growing up in England, the Nazis saw to the fulfillment of Hitler's prophecy of January 30, 1939, when he predicted "the destruction of the Jewish race in Europe."[6] Most of Western Europe fell to the Germans in 1940, the year when dozens of ghettos were set up in the East, as per Security Police Chief Reinhard Heydrich's directive. On May 1, 1940, the Łódź Ghetto was sealed; the longest standing of all the ghettos, Łódź was not liquidated until August 1944. On November 15, 1940, the largest and most infamous of all the ghettos was sealed: the Warsaw Ghetto. Nearly a year later, on October 10, 1941, the ghetto at Terezín, or Theresienstadt, was set up not far from Prague. On July 8, 1943, Milena's family entered that ghetto to await deportation to Auschwitz-Birkenau.

In the same month that Theresienstadt was made into a ghetto, the killing facility at Auschwitz-Birkenau was established. Five other murder camps were also erected across Poland in rapid succession: Chelmno went into operation in December 1941, Sobibor and Blezec in March 1942, Majdanek in May, and Treblinka in June. By the time the killing facilities were up and running, the *Einsatzgruppen,* or killing units, had been at work ever since the Nazis' invasion of Russia, on June 22, 1941. Already they had murdered more than 1.5 million Jews (some estimates run as high as 2.5 million and more) at such infamous killing fields as

Ponary, in Lithuania, and Babi Yar, in the Ukraine. On July 22, 1942, one day after Milena's mother, Anna, wrote her last letter to her little girl, the massive deportations from the Warsaw Ghetto to Treblinka began. Soon the trains were pulling into all six of the murder camps from points near and far. Soon the body of Israel began its ascent on columns of smoke into the sky that would be its cemetery.

Milena's family was not selected for deportation from Theresienstadt to Auschwitz-Birkenau until September 1943. Although uprisings in Treblinka on August 2 and in Sobibor on October 2 of that year resulted in the closure of those camps, Auschwitz-Birkenau was working to capacity until the revolt of the Sonderkommando (crematoria workers), on October 7, 1944. Milena's mother had been murdered six months earlier, on March 8, 1944.

SOME IMPLICATIONS

Those of us who live in a post-Auschwitz world—whose bread now has an ashen taste because it comes from an ashen earth—have been so tainted by the shadow of Auschwitz that many of us can hear the word *Kindertransport* without a shudder. It means "transport of *children.*" Think of it: these children are not on some outing or holiday, not off to visit anyone or even to flee some natural disaster. No, it is a transport of children because if they stay in their homes with their mothers and fathers, they will most certainly be murdered by people whose chief aim is to murder Jewish children.

According to the laws that govern the Nazis' concentrationary universe, *it is illegal for Jewish children to be alive.* If they are to stay alive, they must be orphaned before their mothers and fathers have been murdered. They must be torn from their families, from their names, and from their mother tongue, so that if they are to be, they must not be who they are. Uprooted from their homes, they are utterly homeless, so that if they are to have a place, they must be forever out of place. Severed from their teachings and traditions, from the memory of millennia, if they are to have a future, they must have no past. One sees how the gravitational field of the anti-world extends even to the

British Isles and holds the children of the Kindertransport firmly in its orbit.

Three years after the Kindertransport came to a halt, because of the outbreak of war, other massive deportations were just beginning. Children were among the first selected for those transports, too. Indeed, Adam Czerniakow, head of the Jewish Council in the Warsaw Ghetto, took his own life when the deportations from the Warsaw Ghetto began because, as he stated it, "the Germans want me to kill children with my own hands."[7] The day designated for the deportations from the Warsaw Ghetto to begin was July 22, 1942. It corresponded with Tisha B'Av on the Jewish holy calendar, the day commemorating the destruction of both the First and Second Temples. Later, *Churban,* the term used to refer to the destruction of the Temple, would also be used to refer to the Holocaust.

According to the ancient Jewish sages, when the Babylonians destroyed the First Temple and took away the priests and the Levites, the Shekhinah, the Indwelling Presence of the Holy One, nonetheless continued to dwell in Jerusalem: the Holy City was still holy. But when they took away the children, the Shekhinah herself went into exile: emptied of the children, the Holy City was no longer holy. In the Kindertransport, then, we have the first stage in a long process by which Europe was drained of whatever holiness it might have had. If, as the Jewish tradition teaches, the world is sustained thanks to the breath of little children, the Kindertransport is the first stage of the crumbling of that earth from under the feet. Says Elie Wiesel, "It was as though the Nazi killers knew precisely what children represent to us. According to our tradition, the entire world subsists thanks to them."[8] Certainly the entire world of a mother or a father subsists thanks to them. The moment Anna Roth put her little one on the train bound for England, her world must have started to unravel.

Knowing that in all likelihood they would never see their children again, mothers and fathers placed them on the trains bound for England in order to save their lives. Forced to empty their lives of their children, they were already being drawn into the anti-reality that the Nazis were constructing for them. For part of fashioning the landscape of the concentrationary universe entailed the creation of realms utterly *void of Jewish children.* Simon Wiesenthal, for example, recalls the regular "raids on the children" in the Lvov Ghetto, until there were no children left to raid.[9] And on June 10, 1942, in his diary from the Warsaw Ghetto, the great historian and archivist Emmanuel Ringelblum wrote that in the past, "even in the most barbaric times, a human spark glowed in the rudest heart, and children were spared. But the Hitlerian beast is quite different. It would devour the dearest of us, those who arouse the greatest compassion—our innocent children."[10]

When a Jewish child has to lose her identity in order to save her life, as Milena Roth did, she is shaken not only as a Jew but also as a child. And when a Jewish mother has her child taken from her—even if the little one is taken to a place of safety—she is shaken not only as a Jew but also as a mother. Reading Milena Roth's book, we realize that parallel to the Nazi assault on the child is an assault on the mother. Here too the Jewish tradition opens our eyes to the tearing of the soul that characterizes the Holocaust. According to a traditional teaching in Exodus 19:3, the "House of Jacob" mentioned in that verse refers to the mothers of Israel, whereas the "Children of Israel" designates the men. And the House of Jacob is mentioned first because it is only through the mothers among the Israelites that the Torah comes into the world. Hence, in the Talmud, that encyclopedic collection of Jewish law and lore, it is written that blessing comes to a home only through the wife and mother of the household.

In the phenomenon of the Kindertransport, then, we see the Nazi assault on the Jew unfold as an assault on child and mother. For the Jew in Nazi Europe, birth itself, both for the child and for the mother, was a capital crime. "This conjunction of birth and crime is a *novum* in history," Emil Fackenheim rightly observes. "The very concept of holiness, is the implication, must be altered in response to the conjunction, unprecedented in the annals of history, of 'birth' and 'crime.'"[11] This conjunction of birth and crime is implied by the very existence of the Kindertransport. And it belongs to the very essence of the concentrationary universe that Milena escaped.

Her mother, however, did not escape. The one comfort that Anna

Roth had was that her daughter would not accompany her into a mass grave or gas chamber. Therefore, she could somehow find the words to go into these letters, no matter how agonizing it must have been for her to write them. If she had the courage to write them, we must find the courage not only to read them but also to pursue their ramifications. These letters are made of words that come from a woman as she was swallowed up in the whirlwind. They speak to her little girl and others of life, even as the one speaking is about to slip into death. That is why they are lifesaving letters: not because they saved the mother's life but because they saved Milena's life by attesting to the dearness of life in very simple but very powerful ways. That is why they just might save our lives.

DAVID PATTERSON
The University of Memphis

NOTES

1. Cited in Franklin Littell, *The Crucifixion of the Jews* (Macon, Ga.: Mercer University Press, 1986), pp. 27–28.

2. Immanuel Kant, *The Conflict of the Faculties,* tr. Mary J. Gregor (New York: Abaris, 1979), p. 95.

3. See G.W.F. Hegel, "The Spirit of Christianity and Its Fate," in *Early Theological Writings,* tr. T. M. Knox (Chicago: University of Chicago Press, 1948), pp. 201–5.

4. See Guenther Neske and Emil Kettering, eds., *Martin Heidegger and National Socialism,* tr. Lisa Harries (New York: Paragon, 1990), p. 13.

5. Alfred Rosenberg, *Race and Race History and Other Essays,* ed. Robert Pais (New York: Harper & Row, 1974), pp. 131–32; italics added.

6. Cited in Lucy S. Dawidowicz, *The War against the Jews, 1933–1945* (New York: Bantam Books, 1976), p. 106.

7. See Adam Czerniakow, *The Warsaw Diary of Adam Czerniakow,* ed. Raul Hilberg, Stanislaw Staron, and Josef Kermisz, tr. Stanislaw Staron et al. (New York: Stein and Day, 1979), p. 70.

8. Elie Wiesel, *A Jew Today,* tr. Marion Wiesel (New York: Random House, 1978), pp. 178–79.

9. Simon Wiesenthal, *The Sunflower: On the Possibilities and Limits of Forgiveness,* ed. Harry James Cargas, tr. H. A. Pichler (New York: Schocken Books, 1997), p. 44

10. Emmanuel Ringelblum, *Notes from the Warsaw Ghetto,* ed. and tr. Jacob Sloan (New York: Schocken Books, 1974), pp. 293–94.

11. Emil L. Fackenheim, *The Jewish Bible after the Holocaust* (Bloomington: Indiana University Press, 1990), p. 87.

PREFACE

The letters that form the heart of this volume have been in my possession since I was quite young, well before I left my foster home at sixteen. My foster mother had handed them over to me, stuffed in a large envelope, saying only, "You'd better have these." They were not new to me; I'd read them before, and I was aware that my mother was unique in being held high in my foster mother's esteem, which reinforced my feeling that she had been very special. I do hope they are all that were received, but I have no means of knowing. My foster mother tended to keep correspondence—even her own responses, as evidence in case of quarrels—but no record of her replies to my mother was kept, as far as I know. All my mother's letters were in English except for the single one addressed to me and dated 30 November 1940—over a year after I had left my parents' home in Prague and arrived in England. That letter, written in Czech, was translated for me by a friend many years later.

The existence of these letters had always been deeply important to me, and I would read them at intervals, always because they made my mother seem nearer and also more real: there was the danger that she and all the old life could disappear into unreality. I can still remember very clearly what she looked like, and her letters helped my shaky self-esteem, being a reminder of how valuable I was to her and my father. But I didn't think at all about the letters' chronology or their historic significance. It is lucky that my mother dated them at all, as no envelopes remain.

So the letters traveled around with me each time I moved, but until relatively recently they remained simply an important link with her. It didn't occur to me to put them together in book form until about two years before I started to work on them, in 1999. One day, after rereading them yet again, I noted the dates they covered and realized for the first time, and for no particular reason, what a marvelous and valuable story they made. And by then they did not need to stand alone, for I now knew much more of the story, of which they had become both the starting point and the center.

Because I had no experience of editing, my approach was naive; her narrative was so clear and fresh, its historical significance now manifest, that the idea of tampering with it didn't occur to me. I simply copied the letters verbatim, punctuation and all. But spelling mistakes I copied just once, to spare the reader irritation. The only omissions (which I have noted where they occur) were repetitious administrative details about my forthcoming escape to England, which she was desperately trying to bring about. Where a word or phrase was really muddled, I clarified; but this need was rare.

The spontaneity with which the letters were written is self-evident. Some were typed, some handwritten, with crossings-out, bits added in handwriting, and so on. Several have little drawings in the margins. They are all easy to read but not particularly tidy. Not everyone had typewriters then, and letters tended to be "dashed off" (that is, unless they were to be formal, in which case extreme care was taken), rather as we do e-mail now—with blithe disregard for errors or neatness. You were favored if you received a typewritten letter; not very many people could type at all, so mistakes really did not matter. All sorts of paper had been used: my parents' office paper, with its printed headings; large, flimsy (now transparent and fragile) airmail sheets; small stiff conventional writing paper—anything, it seems, that came to hand.

Apart from the letters' charm and historic value, I felt the story should be recorded for several other reasons. I'd never read anything similar in all the Holocaust literature I've studied. The completeness of the story, with its corroborative details supplied by other witnesses. The normal life first. The account of her striving to get our family to safety—in itself unique, to my knowledge. The success and the failure. The whole aftermath, bad and good, with its redeeming features. I wanted to discuss the matter of recovery from such serious childhood traumas, and the factors that seemed to me to make recovery possible. And finally the record of her heroism in the face of defeat and death.

In my story I have used real names for all the Czechs except the anti-Semitic man's family. All the English people involved have pseudonyms except those who are already well known for their various achievements, and two friends who prefer their real names to be used. All the towns and regions of England except for London have been changed.

ACKNOWLEDGMENTS

Acknowledgment and thanks to Zdena Hermann for her letter of 1996, which is used in chapter 1; for part of a letter in chapter 6; for information from her unpublished family memoir and general family information; and for her translation of the article in the Prague Jewish Yearbook of 1997 *(Zidovská obec v Praze).*

To Helena Milek-Grant for giving me the article in the Prague Jewish Yearbook of 1997, and for general help and family information.

To Lida Vohryzek for her anecdote about my parents' visit to her family in Prague after the war started.

To the Prague Jewish Yearbook of 1997 for the article titled "The Anti-Nazi Struggle of the Czech Jews in Terezin."

To Eva and Ruda Roden for permission to quote from their book *Lives on Borrowed Time* about the gassing of our family at Auschwitz, and for all other information given.

To Eugen Stein for permission to show the family tree he drew up.

I want to thank everyone who was involved with this book.

Nikki Abraham said, "Start at six A.M." when I said I had no time to write it, which is what I did henceforth.

Helena Milek-Grant made it a matter of conscience when she handed me the passage from the Prague Jewish Yearbook of 1997 commemorating my grandfather and mother.

Patrick Gallagher saw that the story should have a good home and gave it its first impetus, well beyond any call of duty.

My husband, children, and friends gave practical help, encouragement, and, above all tolerance, while everyone at the University of Washington Press saw it through the long haul. Naomi Pascal, Xavier Callahan, and all the others I haven't met, thank you.

Lifesaving Letters

1
Introduction

London 26.9.96.

My dear Milena,

Yesterday I have seen the play 'Kindertransport' in the Vaudeville theatre in the Strand, and I thought of you the whole time, as there were many similarities between what was happening on the stage and what happened, unfortunately, to you. I think you must have heard about the play, but if not, I will enclose a leaflet. That does not mean that I reccommend you to see it—it might be too harrowing. On the other hand you might have seen it already, and in that case, I'd like to hear what you thought of It If you can bear to talk about it. I was very moved. Pity its in the wrong language.

I can well remember the little girl that you were when you arrived. I went to collect you from Liverpool Street Station. You were standing all alone, not with the other children, and your face was smeared with 36 hours of dirt and smut from the train combined with traces of tears. Now it all came back to me, together with a straight fawn little coat you wore. What a helpless little girl; I think I can appreciate those feelings better now than then, when I was much more optimistic in all respects, in spite of the difficult situation we were all in.

I took you 'home', which was one tiny attic room in a boarding house in Fitzjohn's Avenue, and you stayed with us for 3 days to get 'acclimatised'. I remember cooking an English breakfast, and getting hair in the eggs, (because the 'kitchen' was in one part of a cupboard, and the 'bathroom' (i.e. basin with shelf for combs etc) in the other part.

Then I took you for walks and showed you advertisements, (notices in shops) for milk, butter, bread, meat, chairs, thus trying to teach you the words. But it was all very sad. Then I took you by train to your new guardians. I was impressed by the big house, (after the Prague flats, not to speak of the room in the boarding house)—it was huge. The dining room table, too, seemed enormous. Jane took you upstairs and you seemed to be quite taken with her and everything, and I was glad of it. That was only the beginning of course.

Love, Zdena

This letter was written to me by my Aunt Zdena, my mother's youngest sister, in September 1996, fifty-seven years after the arrival she describes. In 1939, I was six and a half, and I was packed off on a train from Prague, crammed in with many other children, to save my life from Hitler and his men, who wanted to get us all. I was aware of this; I don't know how. Maybe it was explicitly stated, maybe I absorbed it by osmosis. I knew I would die if I didn't go. There was an atmosphere of terror around me. It seeped into my mind from the old people. They seemed to huddle together, whispering. These trains have come to be known as the Kindertransport, and the journey was arranged because of people and events I didn't fully understand. The trains didn't have a name then, as far as I knew.

Aunt Zdena and her brand-new young husband arrived in Britain very soon after Hitler marched into Prague, on March 16, 1939. They came to England and France on their honeymoon, and he had the sense to start looking for work in London. She was a social worker and wanted to go back to Prague, to her job. Maybe she just couldn't face the facts at first, but by March 30 she returned to London and her husband, having realized that there was no safety in life there. The Czech border was closed on April 1.

On September 16, 2003, a life-size bronze statue of a little girl will be unveiled at Liverpool Street Station in London. It is modeled on the granddaughter of one of the children who came on those trains between March and August 1939. We ranged in age from babes in arms to seventeen years, and although we didn't know it at the time, 10,000 children altogether made the journey to safety during those hectic last months. My train was from Prague, from which only 669 children escaped. At least 5,000 Czech children were left behind, and most were murdered. Others came from all the other European countries that Hitler planned to clear of Jews. I don't know what the other children thought about the reasons they were being sent away from home, but I certainly knew it was a matter of life and death, and my parents told me they would follow later. Some parents may have hoped to see their children again, but many held no illusions.

A huge transparent suitcase is being placed in front of the statue, to symbolize what we brought with us from our old life and what we left behind. Our suitcases became a powerful symbol to us over the years; they and their contents were all we had. Now, to commemorate ourselves at that time, as well as the love that impelled our parents to send us off to safety alone, we have each been asked to put a small memento inside this display. Maybe a toy or book kept through all these years, or a letter from a mother to give a child strength for what was to come. I've chosen a small embroidered pillowcase. I can remember my mother and me packing my suitcase together, and in the year 2000, without a handle, battered and rusty, and with its large, roughly painted green number on the outside, it found a permanent home in the new Holocaust Exhibition at the Imperial War Museum in London.

Sixty years after the period marked by the statue and the museum exhibition, such memorials seem almost a miracle. They are more than a commemoration; they signify a huge shift in attitude.

When we left Prague, we were traveling to an anti-Semitic country in an anti-Semitic world. Britain was the only place to open its doors just this tiny bit, to allow us children to enter, but it did so with provisos and a certain grudging benevolence. If leading Jews had not put pressure on Home Secretary Samuel Hoare in Parliament, it wouldn't have happened at all. The rest of the British population, with some shining exceptions, held attitudes that we would now think of as very backward indeed. To be absolutely honest, the country was xenophobic and racist.

In Britain there was a very special atmosphere, a feeling, directed at us and about us. We were not in danger of being killed, but people spoke about us behind their hands. I have to strain to remember it now, the feeling that there was something smutty, dirty, about us. I heard people discussing Jews—they leaned toward one another, heads a bit closer than usual, voices a bit lowered, "She's Jewish, you know," implying unclean, disgraceful. This feeling lingers, though I feel I should have overcome it by now, and I'm still cautious with strangers, particularly people who seem prejudiced or judgmental (or uneducated), still half in hiding, still a bit afraid of being whispered about with hostility or suspicion. Being whispered about is horrible. Now my hiding is a habit, not a necessity, and depends on the company.

I first noticed a change in the early eighties, when I saw an article in the Sunday *Times* that referred to Jews just in passing, writing of us as if we were ordinary people. That was new. Before, we were not mentioned at all. Next, a young friend in her late thirties asked me what was wrong with the Jews. Why was anyone against them? she wondered. It was a mystery to her; she knew nothing, and felt nothing, against Jews. I realized then that there must actually be many people like her. Attitudes had changed. But my feelings of wariness and discomfort, like my tendency to hide, didn't go away; they'd become a habit.

We came to Britain because Hitler was determined to kill us for being Jewish. The Germans had already invaded Czechoslovakia, and many Jewish families had fled to anywhere they could, but there was little welcome for them around the world. Most countries closed their doors; they feared the Jews would take their businesses. The Jews were suspect. But the British government did allow these 10,000 unaccompanied Jewish children to enter. Theoretically, we were supposed to be in transit to somewhere else, but in any case, we each had to have a guarantor: someone to pay our fare and accept responsibility for us until we were eighteen. The Germans agreed to let this number of children out if those conditions were met. A few adults were also allowed to leave, but only if they accepted menial jobs, ones that the British did not want—domestic work, nursing mental patients, and so on. But most of us children came alone. Our journey happened as a result of our parents' foresight and struggle and because unseen powers relaxed their rules, making a crack just wide enough to let us through.

2
Family History

When you spread out the family tree on my mother's side, it's huge. There are Jacobs and Rosalies, Josefs and Annas, Karolinas and Katerinas, Kamila, Ernst, Siegfried, Ella, Villem, Hermina, and Eduard. A total of 131, and still counting.

But when you look closely, you see that "K.Z." has been marked next to twenty-six of these names, and next to twenty-four of them there is a cross. Those marks appear in the fourth and fifth generations of this seven-generation record. The "K.Z." stands for "concentration camp," which is where those family members met their premature ends, either murdered by gas in Auschwitz or killed in some other way in one of the other camps. And that's where I would have ended up, along with the million and a half other children murdered in the Holocaust, had I not, partly by chance but mostly through the efforts of my mother and several other people, been sent to England on the Kindertransport.

The large family—my grandfather was the eldest of six—is said to have been very close knit, but who can tell. In sentimental hindsight, it's easy to say that it was true. I'd like to think so. They lived in Prague or areas nearby, particularly the ancient town of Tabor or surrounding villages. My great-grandfather and his brother married two sisters. Thus the closeness grew and proliferated into a great network of aunts, uncles, and cousins. But all of that is a legend to me, as I am the youngest and only survivor of my generation. In fact, I now realize that I grew up more alone than anyone in my entire family history.

Another phenomenon is that my own elder daughter is the fifth gen-

Viteslav and Marie Stein, my maternal grandparents, with baby Anna (my mother), about 1906.

eration of eldest daughters. In other words, I am the eldest (and only) daughter of an eldest daughter of an eldest daughter of an eldest daughter. Studies have shown that eldest children are different, and people have different expectations of them, compared to younger siblings. Certainly in my family the eldest had to be strong and take the lead, but whether that was because of nature or circumstances, it's hard to say. We also have at least three generations of orphans. My mother's mother, my mother and her sisters, and I were all young when we lost our parents. I was the youngest. Thus sadness and strength grew out of these losses and early responsibilities. But the family was not mournful by nature, I am certain. We all have a bounce and high spirits not in keeping with our circumstances. There are records of constant family get-togethers and parties, and every family member had intense enthusiasms, hobbies, and skills. I've always felt it was a good heritage in spite of everything. Perhaps it's partly what got me through. That, plus very good parents.

My mother, Anna, was the eldest of three daughters of Viteslav and Marie Stein. Viteslav and Marie, too, had responsibilities, even before assuming those of marriage, since they were the eldest children in their own families.

Viteslav had six younger siblings, four sisters and two brothers, and the family lived above its shop in a village near Tabor, outside Prague. They made a reasonable living from the shop, it seems, and in any case there was always food to be had in the country during hard times. As a young man, Viteslav really had wanted to be a lawyer, and he obviously had the interests of an intellectual. His chief passions seem to have been politics, current affairs, literature, classics, and history. Above all, he was a fervent member of the Social Democratic Party and devoted much energy and time to the group. But he clearly hated extremes, liking neither the Imperial Austro-Hungarian Empire, of which at that time the future Czechoslovakia was a part, nor the extreme left of his own party that eventually broke away to form a Communist wing. He took part in demonstrations, was arrested after one, and spent three nights in prison. A noble deed for the cause.

Despite these intellectual and political interests, Viteslav had to make a living. He did not really like to think of himself as a businessman; nevertheless, it was necessary. It is thought that he worked at first for someone else and then branched off on his own, selling nail studs for soldiers' boots. With the end of the First World War, there was presumably less call for these nails, and a large consignment of boots was lost on the Italian border, so he acquired a new machine for processing horsehair and began importing, processing, and selling this material to other firms for use in upholstered furniture. It seems that this business prospered until the worldwide trade slump of the thirties, and he maintained his political activities and general cultural interests as well.

Viteslav finally got his chance to do what he wanted and pursue his political interests full-time when he was offered the position of manager at the *Social Democrat Press,* becoming in effect its director and editor as well as writing articles for it. This offer coincided with several events in his favor. He was tired of working at something that was not his first priority, he was fifty-five, and my own father, Emil, had just lost his job with Fernet Branca, either because of the financial difficulties of the thirties or because the firm ceased importing the liqueur in which it specialized, making him available to fill Viteslav's place. The family achieved its wish that my parents take over the business. It's hard to know whether this was a mutual decision or whether Viteslav's mother was the dominant force, for this had apparently long been her plan for her son's eldest daughter, my mother, Anna. Whether it was what my parents wanted is another matter, but in those times, I suppose, all jobs were welcome. Anna and Emil were left to struggle with an ailing firm in a bad financial and political climate.

I did know my grandfather. But "know" is a strong word, as I never remember him actually speaking to me. Surely he must have done. Once I remember standing at his elbow, but I have no memory of any conversation. In the last photo taken of our family together, we are at a table in a park; we are having a drink on a warm July Sunday; it was a few days before I left Prague and the family for good, and it is exactly sixty years ago to the day that I write this. It all looks so normal. My mother in a jaunty hat and a smart thirties dress. Myself frowning into the sun; my grandfather, quite bald, sitting sideways, and my father smoking a cigar. It looks so normal, yet it was a historic occasion. They all knew how dire things were; even I did. Surely he must have spoken to me. Why does one forget some things and not others?

In October of that year, only three months after I left for England, Grandfather took part in an anti-Nazi demonstration in Prague. That was a very brave thing to do. He was arrested, and in February of the next year the family heard that he had died of "dysentery" in the concentration camp at Oranienberg. His friend Karel Pakowsky wrote, "Viteslav Stein, former Editor of our Trades Union paper, was the first of the leading men of the organization who perished." He was sixty-two years old and had been perfectly fit.

Grandfather Viteslav Stein, Anna, me, and Emil, July 1939, shortly before I left for England. This is the last photo taken of my family.

I wish I'd known my mother's mother, Marie. She died of cancer three weeks before I was born. Yet I feel as if I can imagine her. I have so many of the lovely things she made. Lace tablecloths, seven of them, and in particular the "special" cloth, which she made for each of her three daughters, possibly intended for the wedding dowry and breakfast. That is what we have used it for, for my own and my elder daughter's weddings, and I expect my mother put it to the same use. It is still there, ready for the next occasion. These material things become so important, perhaps too important, because the people themselves are missing. It is all we have of them. But we should not forget their other legacy, one of motherhood and caring for their own. That is passed on, too, as it certainly was to me.

Yet this grandmother seemingly had so little. Her father was said to have been the black sheep of the family, and he did not provide for Marie and her two younger brothers. He may or may not have died young or deserted them—it's not clear—so their mother had to support her family with what she could earn at a market stall in the village of Beroun, selling textiles and hosiery in the main square.

I feel a sense of outrage for all those generations (including my own) that were denied proper and adequate schooling. You have only to look at the history of some families: children removed from school at thirteen or fourteen, deemed by mean-spirited governments or the social systems of the day to be fit only for menial and low-paying jobs, their entire lives blighted by overwork and unused abilities. Give them enough education, and they rise straight into the professions, if that's what they want. This happened again and again in my own and many other families. My grandmother Marie was schooled only until she was fourteen and then spent years as an apprentice at a dressmaker's salon until she finally was prepared to open a little salon of her own. But her brother Hugo somehow won scholarships, or was helped to stay in school, and at once rose to become a doctor. Straight from a village market stall to medicine. Girls, of course, were the second ones to get a chance.

While Marie was working at her own salon, her mother died, also of cancer, and she was left to do all she could to help her two brothers with their training and education. She was therefore responsible for that little family, which she must have supported with the earnings from her salon.

I do not know how my grandparents met, or even what my grandfather's first job was. They did have a fairly hard time during the First World War, suffering food shortages like most of the people in Prague and living in a flat that was far from labor-saving. The food had to be foraged from all sorts of sources in the country, and as if that weren't enough, it was taxed when it was brought into Prague. Their apartment was at the top of a tall building without an elevator, so everything had to be brought up by hand. The babies, the pram, the food, wood for the stove. And the laundry had to go down to the basement washing room and up again to the attic to dry. Maids were poorly paid in those days, so my grandmother could afford to keep one, but she still worked very hard.

Despite her limited education and even deprivation of care, I'm told Marie became wise and knowledgeable in many things and was a warm and loving mother to her three daughters. She ran her home beautifully, being so good with her hands, and her standards were high. In their second apartment, which, again, Viteslav chose, they lived on the fourth floor, without an elevator, in a three-room flat on the edge of a park, with a good view of the trees from the balcony, and this is where my mother spent twenty years of her life. The girls all shared one room, which was used as a dining and family room during the day. Yet they regularly had big gatherings, with friends coming to visit and eat around the table.

Although, according to Aunt Zdena, Viteslav took his wife's homemaking skills somewhat for granted, he nevertheless seemed to have a respect for her brains, and the home was filled with political and general discussions of every kind. Marie and all three of her daughters were feminists, and Marie had taken part in marches in her youth, campaigning, naturally, among other things, for the vote for women. Not one of the girls had the benefit of her presence when they had their own babies; she died of cancer in her fifties, but at least she was spared all that came after.

On my father Emil's side of the family, things are both clearer and more obscure. Clearer because my relationship with my grandmother is so vivid; more obscure because my data are so sparse. This is because, up till now, I know of no relation on my father's side who survived. Lately I have realized that there may be, somewhere in the world—perhaps in Alexandria, Egypt, where my father and his sister were brought up—descendants of my grandparents' siblings who might have been spared the Holocaust because they were not in Europe. But the problem is, I don't know if my father's parents had any siblings. We are doing a search on the Internet and in the Czech Republic, but I have only two family surnames: Baum, my paternal grandmother's maiden name, and Bernard, a businessman who is said to have been quite successful, in Alexandria, I believe. And that is all I know.

But I do know a little about my father's family. His parents came from Slovakia but met in Italy. I don't know why they were there or why they moved to Alexandria and set up in business, and I don't know what kind of business it was. At any rate, the family seems to have done well enough to send both Emil and his sister Lisa to the French lycée, where they got their qualifications in both commerce and languages. The family moved back to Prague in about 1920, when people of German and Austrian origin were obliged by Egypt to return to their homelands after the First World War. Slovakia was part of Austria-Hungary at that time, and the family returned to Prague. Emil was employed as an accountant with the Italian firm of Fernet Branca, where he used his wide range of languages, and Lisa worked as a multilingual secretary.

My paternal grandfather, Morič Roth, is a blank, since he died before I could know him, and no one can tell me anything about him. But my grandmother is a beacon memory of my childhood. Recently I've learned that she came originally from Russia. She was all that a grandmother should be. Soft, wide, and loving. In her eyes I was perfect, and memories of her helped sustain me when things got bad. When I was good, she gave me a penny, and when I wasn't, I got two pennies. I understood perfectly well that this wasn't meant to encourage me to be bad but to console me for having lost control of my less-good self. I knew she loved me with all my faults, but the faults weren't encouraged by the spoiling. Of course I didn't analyze it at the time. I just wallowed in her love, and I was free to take it for granted then.

Grannie lived in a small house in Hloubětín, outside Prague. I say the house was small, and in my memory it was, but when I, as her ultimate heir, looked through the details many years later, after it had been expropriated first by the Germans and then the Communists, I saw that it was a house of several apartments. These apartments would have contained tenants from whom she must have collected rent. At any rate, we used to travel by tram to visit her every Sunday, and this was a great joy to me. She had a garden, and whether I'd been good or bad, I got the traditional gift of almonds and raisins, in a small cone of stiff brown paper, to gobble up as I saw fit.

Everything in the garden might not have been quite so lovely as it

Sarena Rothová. This is the only surviving photo of my maternal grandmother.

looked to me. Auntie Lisa lived with Grannie and perhaps would have preferred to have a husband. There is a story of an unhappy love affair. A man she had set her heart on let her down, or something like that; I don't know any more. There is also a hint of some emotional tyranny in a letter from my mother, in which she mentions that Lisa did not go away for a holiday "as Grannie might be lonely." I remember my aunt as not a happy person. Such clues make me feel that modern rebellions may have been overdue.

Grannie was also unwell. In the only photo I have of her, she fills a shapeless dress, her hairdo is what you might call simple, and her hands look a bit swollen. In those days it was called dropsy, heart trouble. She's in her garden, sitting under a tree beside what looks like a chicken coop (and I know she did keep chickens), and when I look closely, I see she wasn't all that old, maybe in her early fifties, although naturally she looked old to me. I can't even imagine the scene when they hauled her off. For years I fooled myself into thinking that she died a natural death, of heart failure, even though I had the documents showing that she went to Auschwitz. It seems too outrageous to believe. This lady, like all the others, living in the country, minding her own business. And Europe had to be rid of her?

In 1989, after the peaceful Czech revolution, I visited Hloubětín with my husband. We took the no. 5 tram, which looked old enough to be the same one that had run all those years ago, and we had the number of the house. But the houses were not numbered chronologically along the street, but according to the order in which they'd been built. We were recovering from flu at the time, and it was windy and wintry, and also a hilly place, so after a lot of searching and even asking at the local school, we had to give up. I really would have loved to see that house again.

Our family, although Jewish on both sides, was not observant in any way. I'm told that Viteslav occasionally went to synagogue to please his parents, but all attendance died out with him. It was the same on my father's side; I never heard or saw anything Jewish in the way of religion in Grannie's house either. However, I have a distant memory of visiting a synagogue in Prague on the Day of Atonement and seeing people sniffing oranges stuck with cloves, to support their energies while they fasted. And once, I believe, I was the youngest at a Passover meal. We didn't live in a particularly Jewish part of Prague, nor were my parents' friends only Jewish. In fact, all my mother's friends in England and those to whom she sent me were churchgoing Christians.

Although Anna was the eldest of the three daughters of Viteslav and Marie Stein and I've been told that she may have been the most gifted, even the most favored, of the three, it's a strange thing that she was the one who got the raw deal and was denied the higher education she desperately wanted. I have a theory that it may have been because she was the replacement child for the elder brother, Jiri, who died in early babyhood, and she was expected to carry on the family business as a boy would have done.

Losing Jiri must have been so hard for Marie, this responsible young

The three Steinová sisters: Zdena, Milada, and Anna.

woman who was without parents herself. It happened in the first years of the twentieth century, when prenatal and postnatal care hardly existed. Advice about baby care was passed down from mothers and older relatives, and Marie had no one to help her. She didn't have enough milk, and no one advised her to feed her baby supplementary food, so he just didn't thrive. At that time, the infant mortality rate was high all over the world, from infection as well as inadequate feeding. So in order to preserve the life of her second baby, Anna, Marie went to the mountains in Prichovice, in the hills above Tannwald, where her brother Hugo, a country doctor, had his practice. And it was he who saved my mother's life, by instructing his sister how to prepare sterile supplementary food, and it is thus to him, in a way, that I and my little family branch owe our existence.

As a child, Anna is said to have been mischievous and not very kind to her middle sister, Milada. But she got away with a lot by looking innocent. This characteristic doesn't seem to have continued, for later she was all kindness and decency. But between those two sisters, jealousy did continue for some years. From the earliest age, Anna was exceptionally lively, interested in everything. The real trouble came when she wanted to go to the gymnasium (high school) to prepare for university. She wanted to study astronomy and mathematics, unheard of for a girl. Viteslav's mother stepped in and vetoed the idea, and the family agreed that Anna should study business so that she, with whomever she married, could take over from her father when he retired. Thus were people's, and particularly girls', lives thrown away by others. It also seems odd that, given Viteslav's intellectual interests, the horsehair business should have taken precedence over higher education.

Anna apparently cried and pleaded, but the most she could persuade her parents to allow was that she should study English for a year and then French for another while she was going to business school as they wanted. But nothing kept her from studying. Milada went to the classical gymnasium without opposition, and Anna studied Latin and Greek on her own to keep up with her sister. She took innumerable courses and became proficient at so many things. Her English came up to teaching standard. She learned drawing, painting, and embroidering on silk. I still have the huge, beautiful bird she embroidered onto dark red silk. I had it made into an evening dress, and I and my elder daughter wore it, and now my younger one has it, but the occasions were never grand enough for the dress! Anna painted on china and made a whole set for her mother. She was always full of energy, imagination, and ideas for things to do, organizing outings and journeys with maps and guidebooks.

There was something about her that created a special aura; charisma, we call it now. Her skin was clear, she had a direct gaze, her honesty and sincerity shone through, and there was an intense purpose. She had an infectious gaiety as well, and a maybe slightly mischievous enthusiasm for everything. She had leadership and friendship skills, too, and it was those which attracted the friends she made in England and which eventually saved my life.

After completing the business courses, Anna couldn't postpone going out to work any longer. She was then still only about seventeen but managed to find a job outside the family business. I don't know what it was, but I believe she was able to use her language skills. She tried to fill her spare time and holidays and once again she was up against opposition. She wanted to join the Girl Guides. Heaven knows why this was opposed—maybe, unlike in England, the Guides were not well known in Czechoslovakia—but she got her way and was soon running a troop. Her sisters were able to follow her into the Guides without opposition. It seems she always had to either forge the way or do without. She also took up photography and persuaded her family and friends to buy studio portraits of themselves and their families, and made enough money to cover the costs of her hobby. Cameras were not so common at that time, and she used the old-fashioned type, with a black hood that went over her head to keep out the light.

She had a good business sense altogether, and one year, going on holiday to England, she took a collection of children's clothes designed by a friend, did good business, and sold them all. In another business venture, she organized four friends into a "tennis five," which hired an expensive tennis court and took turns renting it out an hour at a time. When it was Anna's turn to run it, she made more profit than anyone else, and the group was able to have a fine holiday in Switzerland on the proceeds.

This special personality of my mother's was quite evident to me as a child and is not a view in hindsight. That, plus the devoted love she gave me, has been my rock. Both something to be proud of in her, and of inheriting. Something to live up to with pleasure. She even kept a diary, written in Czech, which she sent with me to England. It took many years to get it translated, because it bored everyone to death. She was considered almost too devoted, even to have spoiled me; in this diary she records my every smile and whimper from birth to the age of four. I can understand everyone's boredom, but it was another valuable strength to me. It was so strange to read many years later that I was such a nice child. I had been brainwashed for so many years afterward to believe that I wasn't.

In actual fact, I didn't feel spoiled. My mother's standards were high, and if I fell below them, I had severe reprimands. I didn't wash properly once, or wore my day clothes in bed, or something like that, and I can still feel the disgrace. Even worse, I once told a lie, an unforgivable sin. I had to stand in the corner, face to the wall, for quite a while. I didn't learn to tell even a white lie until I was forty, so successful was her lesson about the need for honesty. Her diary records many occasions when I was disciplined, even with a smack from my father when I was rude. I knew she was devoted to me, not so much through hugs and kisses, which I don't remember at all, but just through the atmosphere of steady interest and devotion.

She was lively but intent and thoughtful in those last years, and now we know what she was thinking about. The underlying gaiety was not so evident; being Jewish in Europe during the thirties was not fun. Yet somehow an air of fear did not hang heavy in our home; that came when the elders gathered together. Then it was terrifying. When they huddled together, whispering (the child mustn't hear), it was as if the miasma of the camps was already swirling toward us. This is what told me that our lives were in danger.

Yet for all the idealism and happy memories, I have to be realistic and remember that our relationship was not tested by adolescence; nor did I have to cope with the pressures of a normal extended family. But I think she would have taught me, as the eldest, to master those. All semblance of normal family life disappeared with my departure. Except for those years in Prague, I don't know what a normal life is. I say that, not meaning that I don't live a normal life now, but that the experiences I have inside and behind me fill my mind with a background that is not normal and must color all my reactions for all of my life.

Even the family life we had was a funny sort of normal life, with her need to struggle for our escape. I don't know what sort of person I would have become in normal circumstances. It's a strange thing, imagining how it would have felt not to have had to spend the second half of life overcoming the events of the first half, and regaining the confidence of my place in the universe that had been lost.

I remember those years before I was seven, very well indeed.

My father was a gentle and lovely father, and as devoted to me as she was. It was quietly expressed, there was nothing loud or show-off about him, and I never remember him doing or uttering a rough or disturbing thing. He talked to me seriously. We sat side by side, on the rather hard utilitarian blue tweed-covered sofa bed that must have been considered modern in Central Europe at that time, facing the big windows at the end of the sitting room while he showed me his papers from work. On one occasion he had a small thick sheaf of color samples, which gave me the idea that he was in the paper-selling business. After supper he might take me for a walk, and I skipped for joy when I saw the lights at night, crossing the bridge over the Vltava River. Ice-cream vendors sold brightly colored cornets, and to see the different ice-cream colors layered on with a wooden paddle, and then reappearing again as one licked the cone, was magic. So were the gingerbread men with colored pictures stuck on their fronts at Christmastime, and the sweets wrapped in multicolored papers with white fringed ends, at around the time of Saint Nicholas. Although I cannot remember seeing the tiny houses in the small winding street near Prague Castle, I think they must have made a deep impression, because when I draw, the houses always look like the ones in Hansel and Gretel. I think that in some ways one matures fast after these experiences; in other ways, I believe, one stays arrested in certain childhood views and attitudes, as for example in the memory of one's parents and surroundings, and in some of one's childish needs that weren't met for long enough.

But when I recount these things, they are memories only of facts, with feelings recalled, but now felt faintly, sometimes with an effort. And when I think about it, fear was never very far away. I feared intruders into the flat. I don't know if the maid ever left me alone while my mother worked, but I would look through the spy hole to see who was outside. I knew better than to answer the doorbell. Hungry people came to the door, and my mother fed them soup, which they ate on the stairs. I remember the frightening bits of fairy tales and films: witches, wolves, hobgoblins.

We lived like most people in Prague, in a flat. Ours was in the 7th district, and I don't think this was a particularly Jewish quarter. I can remember it so clearly: on the second or third floor, dark golden parquet floors; that was very important; it's always the first thing I think of when I remember my home. This is what was imprinted on my mind as the ideal room: the feeling of size, lightness, height; parquet floors, and a soaring view of the road and nearby park as I flew between the two big rooms on a swing fixed by my father in the double doorway. Up I would go until I was level with the glass cases on the wall that housed his tropical fish—black, brown, or colorful yellow or orange. One day a black fish lay heavy and still in the bottom of his glass home. That was my first experience of death.

I remember our life there. Helping my mother sort linen on the black-and-white tiled floor of our hall, and the fun of kicking it around a bit. I slept on a cot or small bed in the sitting part of the front room, and my favorite toy by far was a folding dollhouse made of painted tin. Each room in the house could be taken apart from the others and played with separately. The bathroom was best because it had small tanks on the outside walls, into which you could put water which then flowed out when you turned on the taps inside. Quite recently I saw a replica of this dollhouse in an exhibition of children's toys of the thirties, in Paris. I felt very excited and wanted to shout, "There's my dollhouse!" I cannot remember if I took it to England with me when I left Prague; probably not, as it would have taken up too much room in my suitcase. I remember my mother grinding coffee with a tiny circular handle fastened to the top of a wooden boxlike container that was fastened to the wall in our kitchen. I think European children were allowed to drink coffee, whereas English children were not.

School was a great joy to me. I was extremely sociable. I would invite strange children to be my friends, and I'm not sure if this was done out of loneliness or whether I just wanted to share. I can remember talking to a little girl in a shop and asking her to be my friend. The school lessons were such fun, and they taught us about God, and how He was everywhere. I shoved all the other kids along the bench so that *He* should sit next to *me*. I hung my coat above a sign for a wren. We were vaccinated and had to wear suitable short-sleeved dresses for this purpose on the day of the shots. I can remember walking round the corner to my home afterwards with some of the other children, bare-armed, displaying my scar with pride.

My mother cooked for her youngest sister Zdena's wedding, and in my enthusiasm I fell onto the wood-burning stove and landed on my hand. My Aunt Míla, who was by now a doctor, came and rescued me. I think she too was engaged to be married by then, or soon after, and I took a great liking to her fiancé, Arnošt, and asked him to wait for me to grow up and marry me instead. My hand was a mess for the wedding, swollen under a huge blister and a bandage, which everyone squashed when they shook my hand.

We had birthday parties, all the normal things, and my mother used to set out a particular pale pink, double damask tablecloth, which I later took to England. I learned to skate, my favorite thing; Saturday mornings were dedicated to perfecting my arabesques. On one occasion someone had a bad fall, and the grazed bloody face worried me a lot. Skiing was another matter. I remember being fastened onto my first small skis at the age of three. Immediately I grasped the insanity of weighting down my legs and sliding down precipices. Not for me, never. The rest of the family despised me for this, but not my parents, who accepted my point of view.

I heard discussions about our proposed escape to England. My father was against sending me ahead alone, and I believe that was the only dispute between my parents I ever heard. I can actually remember sitting at our dining table, and the letter they were discussing flew across the table as my mother argued in favor. This must have been the letter that invited me to precede them. I certainly knew we mustn't tell Grannie, because she would have become hysterical to think of my being shipped abroad alone. We had to pretend that I would go to safety in the country, in Tabor, where we had relatives. This was the one exception to pure honesty that my mother allowed.

I remember all the crises. Munich, although I didn't know the name. My mother seemed to be getting in extra supplies. Lamps, fuel, food. I didn't know what it meant, but it's clear in my mind. Then one day the German troops marched into Prague, and I stood at the big windows at the far end of our sitting room and saw the black helmets passing by at right angles to our street, along the main road ahead. My mother said we had been ordered to hang out Czech flags to pretend we were pleased. The radio fascinated me. How did the man who was speaking know he must stop when we turned the switch? I think I have a memory of bad news coming out of that radio.

We made a last visit to Grannie before I left, maintaining the fiction of my destination. We had a drink with my grandfather Viteslav in the park, as we see in the photo, just as if life were normal. But it never was again.

3
The Letters

In 1930, having long since won the battle to join the Girl Guides, my mother led a troop of Brownies and Guides to represent Czechoslovakia at the International Girl Guides Jamboree in England, where the founders, the Baden-Powells, were present. As well as being a sort of ambassador for her home country, she may also have helped increase the Guides' popularity in Czechoslovakia when she returned.

Her troop's regular meetings were on a weeknight to learn various skills, and then at weekends they'd go for a tram or train ride into the country, followed by a long hike. In summer there would be a camp. Quite complicated to organize; no modern tents; I think they must have done everything except actually rub two sticks together to make a fire. According to her sister Zdena's account, it was rugged. Before even starting the journey, the girls would have to get planks to make a base for the tents and gather quantities of equipment, and once they arrived, poles had to be cut to length, a kitchen assembled, latrines dug.

My mother must have been twenty-five when she got this chance to visit England, and it was there that she met the woman who was eventually to try to save our lives and become my foster mother. Because of her striking personality, she made at least four other friends who all agreed to keep in touch after the jamboree. They must all have been inspired by this international meeting, and it stayed in their minds as something special. Among these women, Doris Campbell was at that time the only one who was married, and lived with her husband and three children in the west of England, whereas all four of the others already knew one another in the same town in the Midlands and retained a much closer relationship. I don't know what jobs they had, but at least one was a schoolteacher. They all seemed to think very highly of my mother, and all tried equally hard to help my family escape when things in Europe turned bad.

My mother's first letter to her new English friend was written from her parents' home in Prague. Although she was a working woman, it was normal for girls to remain at home until they married. Apart from any other factor, it would probably have been too expensive for them to live on their own, and in any case, few were so independent at that time.

Doris was married at nineteen to a doctor, and was proud of the social position this gave at that time. It was a financial and social step up for a girl from a very religious Protestant pastor's family, reared frugally under extreme sectarian rules by a mother with limited education and narrow views. Doris was the second of six children, with a favored eldest brother who was given all the advantages. She was yet another girl who was denied a proper education. I don't think my mother knew any of this, but she certainly knew and didn't mind that Doris's was a Christian and religious home. Doris seemed jolly in public, especially when she was young. She was well off enough to leave her children in the care of a nanny while she followed her many interests outside the home. I think my mother and Doris really knew little or nothing about each other, and I'm struck by the superficial nature of the relationship and their letters, and even the formality of their tone. They contrast with the far warmer tone and first-name basis my mother used with her other English friends. I don't know why this was so, as Doris was not really a formal person. Maybe just being married gave people a more formal, and even respected, status at that time.

The letters are all written in English—sometimes typed on an old machine, sometimes handwritten in easy-to-read European script, with lots of corrections and occasionally little drawings in the margin—and begin immediately after their first meeting and before my mother was married in 1931. As the situation in Europe worsened, her letters show her deepening dependence on Doris's goodwill but no deepening in personal knowledge of each other. I don't know how well my mother knew the others, but I have the impression from the letters they wrote that it may have been a very little more.

Pštroska 17
Prague 7
Sept. 20th 1930
Dear Mrs Campbell,

At last I am able to send you the snaps I took at the picnic with you and both your boys with Lord and Lady Baden Powell. I am sending one for each of them, as I think they will like to have them. Isn't the cottage nice? The second one I took on one film with another picnic one, so it looks now as if your heads are looking out of the chimneys. Rather funny, but it was a pitty [*sic*].

I had the English Guiders here and had a most jolly and lovely time. Everyone in the train thought that I was a paid interpreter as they didnt understand any other language than English. But they learnt how to speak most brainily with hands and drawings, etc.

I have a most busy time now, as a lot of work waited for me now after the holidays.

Have organised my whole Girl Guide Company as to the English Patrol System, so I wonder how it will work. I think well. I have learnt very much indeed at the Conference. Must write two articles, and have a talk at a Guider's meeting about it. I hope I didn't forget anything. It would be no wonder, as a) it was too much of it, and b) too much was after it, still.

Your town is a lovely spot, and when now thinking back to it, reminds me somehow of Nice.

It is very late and I must go to bed. So good night. I shall be glad if sometimes you too would send me a line about you and your children.

Yours very sincerely,
Anka[1] Steinová

1. It is common in Czechoslovakia to put a *k* in a name to make it a diminutive—so "Anna" becomes "Anka."

November 7th 1931

Dear Mrs Campbell,

I have been ever so glad when in the morning of my wedding day your letter arrived.

Thank you for all your good wishes. I'll enclose to this letter a photograph so that you see how my husband looks like. He is very nice, and I was engaged to him on the 27th June this year. But I knew him more than a year before and since Christmas we knew that we should be engaged. When I was in England at Foxlease I knew him already, but at that time he was not more to me than a nice gentleman whom I met every week at the French Club. After the engagement I ran a camp of Guides (34 children altogether, I being there for ten days the single Guider there) and when I returned on the 17th July we started to look out for a flat. (we mostly have houses on the flat system in centre of Prague) We have found a very nice flat not exactly in the centre, where the air is not so good, but near to reach the centre of the City and close to a park. I had then of course a mad rush for some months with furniture, curtains, lamps etc, and still now there is not all in order. But we hope it'll be soon.

My husband (as you ask if he is of the same nationality as I am) was born in Alexandria where his father married. But his father derives from the Eastern part of Slovakia, so that then, after the Great War, all foreigners, Germans and Austrians, were obliged to return to their countries, and as you know, Czechoslovakia was before, the part of Austria-Hungary. So they returned to Prague ten years ago.

He speaks French, Italian, Arabic, Czech, German, and English. English I put the last as he doesn't talk it so well as the other languages. You see with languages we quite fit together. He is Jewish as I am. He has been since eight years employed with a commercial firm (Fernet Branca[1]) which needs foreign languages.

My wedding was very lovely. I haven't had white on as I had a civil wedding at the Town Hall. But the Old Town Hall of Prague is such an old place that it makes things very festival like. I had a very light sand coloured dress of crepe-romain and a light fur coat with a small hat on. The hat was dark green velour, very pretty, though perhaps it sounds strange it has matched very well with the light sand colour of the dress. Guiders and

Anna and Emil Roth on their wedding day, November 24, 1931, Prague.

Guides, not many, just a few, formed two lines at the entrance of the hall. It was very nice and somehow very jolly. I wasn't much excited really, only when I had to sign there the name, my hand trembled a little. There were a lot of people present, and everybody said it was a lovely wedding. We could not go for the honeymoon anywhere, as in the office where my husband works they have just most work now before Christmas. But I don't mind at all as 1) I have seen already many countries really. 2) The flat needs still so much work that I rather like to be here and to do it all here myself. I like best when I can do such things myself. I go still to work in my father's office. Every afternoon. In the morning I do some work in the kitchen and make the beds etc.

Also Guides I shall still continue to run. I have quite nice Brownies again, in my Guide Company.

I have been thrilled by your calling your dog Janet 'Boytsam'. Pojdsem[2] is the right spelling. But of course Boytsam is lovely.

It is very kind of you to write me that you will send me a wedding present. Thank you in advance. I shall love it I am sure.

Please say my love to the children. I can think that they are getting already great and tall little people, especially Harry who is in the boarding school. I should just love to see him in the long trausers [*sic*].

With much love, Anka

P.S. My husband doesn't mind at all my remembering all the good friends in England.

and another P.S. on November 24th 1931

Isn't it a shame I haven't yet posted this letter to you. But you must blame it on the photographer who promised us to make the photographs already ten days ago, and he has done it only today. And I had promised you in the letter to send a photo. The photo looks a little serious, as we were in the best humour that day. My flat is already almost arranged, it is becoming very nice.

1. Fernet Branca specialized in drinks of various kinds, in particular a medicinal liqueur, and my father worked there as an accountant.

2. "Pojdsem" is an endearment.

My parents were married at the Old Town Hall in Prague, and I was born in October the following year.

Prague, 4th March, 32

Dear Mrs Campbell,

It is a shame I haven't written to you yet, but as an excuse I only must tell you that only today I have started to answer and thank for Christmas letters and presents from my English friends, and you are just among the first to whom I am writing.

EMIL ROTH
AGENCE · COMMISSION · REPRÉSENTATION
PRAGUE
TCHÉCOSLOVAQUIE

PRAGUE, 4th March
VII, Dobrovského 4

It is a shame I haven't written to you yet but, as an excuse I only must tell you that onl to-day I have started to answer and thank for Christmass ters and presents to my English friends and you are just amongs th first to whom I am writing. This is only a show how madly sy I have been all the last two months. We have every free evening or Sunday afternoon visitors, my numerous aun and uncles and cousins and friends, who come to see us in o new flat. My home is very nice, if you ever would come to Czecho I think you would like it. We have got sunshine from morni till afternoon, it is so joyous to be at home in the morni Excuse my mistakes, but I am thinking quicker than the t writer can write, you know. I have been a little ill all last week, to-day I am all right already, and so I haven been in the office of my father., which means that a lot o work awaits me there to be done. In the morning I cook ne. It is a great fun. I had an idea of cooking before, but of course you can immagine, when I was always in my father office I had no practise. Just occasionally when mother wa not all right or at a guide camp I cooked. And now there a a lot of inventions which I do when I start cooking. To-day I shall make a sort of rice pudding, have made fire already the kitchen stove and after this letter will be finished sh start to cook. We have of course no English fire places, bu in the kitchen a stove with an oven and in the rooms big ti

I hope you'll excuse my typing the letter. Typing is much quicker for me than writing.

tube through smoke goes to the chimney
ovens for baking
a reservoir for hot water
here coal is put in
ash
a kitchen stove

This is only to show how madly busy I have been all the last two months. We have every free evening or Sunday afternoon visitors, my numerous aunts and uncles and cousins and friends, who come to see us in our new flat.

stoves. As to our flat we have got an American heating
stove which is very agreeable as it heats the hole flat
day and night with very little trouble. I intend to make
snaps of my rooms so next time when shall write I hope to send
them to you, if they are successful, so that you can get an
idea how my home looks like.

Oh, am an ape. I did not thank you for the lovely
tray cloth, did I. It arrived as it seems to me just one day
after I have sent off my Xmass wishes. And then we were very
busy before Christmass, and then we were in the mountains
skiing for the Xmas holidays, and so
the letter to you got postponed till now. I love the
tray cloth and was very happy to have got it because I have go
only just one and I wanted another one so urgently. Because
when one got dirty I had no one to put instead. Thank you
much indeed. It is lovely to have things which remind you wi
using them of your friends. You asked me about Xmass. Yes we
too have turkey, and always fish. Fish from the sweet waters/
pike/ which at this time of year are best. We haven't g
any Xmas pudding, (but x mas cakes) but once I have got a small one from a frie
from Sheffield and then I made it myself. She sent me the rec
I have also got as a wedding present an English cookery book
so when I like I can make English custard, puddings, pies etc.
don't hang up stocking, this we do for the St. Niclas d ay (6th Dec) in
country, but in most of the families there is a Christmase
tree, i.e. a fir tree lovely trimmed with cakes, glittering thi
and candles and under the Xmas tree all the presents are to
found. We haven't got holly in our country at all (it does not grow here) and the cus
with hanging up mistletoe we have adopted from England I thi
Now the page is full, it seems, and therefore I
must close my letter. I do hope to get once again some news
from you, and in case the children would be interested of
something to know please do write, I shall be glad to tell the

Yours very sincerely
Anka

Mrs = PANÍ Anka S. Rethová

decorated Xmas tree

My home is very nice, if ever you would come to Czecho. I think you would like it. We have got sunshine from morning to afternoon, it is so joyous to be home in the morning. Excuse my mistakes, but I am thinking quicker than the typewriter can write, you know.

I have been a little ill all the last week, but today am all right already, so I haven't been in the office of my father, which means a lot of work awaits me there to be done. In the morning I cook alone. It is great fun. I had an idea of cooking before, but of course you can imagine, when I was always in my father's office I had no practice. Just occasionally when mother was not all right or at a Guide camp, I cooked. And now there are a lot of inventions that I do when I start cooking. Today I shall make a sort of rice pudding. I have made fire already in the kitchen stove and after this letter will be finished shall start to cook. We have of course no kitchen fireplaces, but in the kitchen a stove with an oven and in the rooms big tile-stoves. As to our flat, we have got an American heating stove which is very agreeable as it heats the whole flat day and night with very little trouble. I intend to take snaps of my rooms, so next time when I shall write I hope to send them to you, if they are successful, so that you can get an idea what my home looks like.

Oh, I am an ape, I did not thank you for the lovely tray cloth, did I. It arrived as it seems to me just one day after I have sent off my Christmas wishes. And then we were very busy before Christmas, and then we were in the mountains skiing for the Christmas holidays, and so the letter to you got postponed till now. I love the tray cloth because I have got only just one, and I have wanted another one so urgently. Because when one got dirty I had no one to put instead. Thank you very much indeed. It is lovely to have things which remind you when using them of your friends.

You asked me about Xmas. Yes, we too have turkey, and always fish. Fish from the sweet waters, carp/pike, which at this time of year are best. We haven't got any Xmas pudding, (but Xmas cakes), but once I got a small one from a friend in England and then I made it myself. She sent me the recipe. I have also got as a wedding present an English cookery book, so when I like I can make English custard, puddings, pies, etc. We don't hang up Xmas stockings, this we do for the St Nicholas Day 6th December, in our country, but in most of the families there is a Christmas tree, i.e. a fir tree lovely trimmed with cakes, glittering things and candles, and under the Xmas tree all the presents are to be found. We haven't got holly in our country at all, (it does not grow here), and the custom with mistletoe we have adopted from England I think. Now the page is full it seems, and therefore I must close my letter. I do hope to get once again some news from you, in case the children would be interested to know something, please do write, I shall be glad to tell them.

Yours very sincerely, Anka

Prague 7

Dobrovského 4

23rd November 1932

Dear Mrs Campbell,

I want to tell you that I have got a daughter. She was born on the third of this month, is very tiny and very sweet.

I have not written to you for a long time, as this year we had a bad time, as my dear mother was very ill and just three weeks before my baby was born she died. You may imagine what a blow it has been for me and for all of us.

Your children will be interested how the baby is called Milena Marie, pronounced like 'inn' and 'get'. Marie = Mary.

With sincere regards,

yours, Anka[1]

1. This was written on a postcard.

12th December 1932

Dear Mrs Campbell,

It has been awfully nice of you to have sent me the lovely coatee for Milena. It is just the small size so she has worn it a lot already, since we have big frosts in our country in the last days, and also before it was rather cold. My baby was very small when she was born; 2.32 Kg = 4.64 lbs! She arrived a bit sooner than she had to. But she is well, growing, weighs now (just today, ten weeks old) 3.9kg, almost 8 pounds. She was eighteen inches long when eighteen days old. (before that she was not measured.) And now she is 24 inches long. Shall send a snap just in the coatee you have sent me, but it is rather dark, I am sorry she does not support the sun shining in her eyes, so the snap does not come out as well as it ought to.

I was in a Sanatorium and it was very nice there. I came to the sanatorium at 2.30am, and 6.30am baby was here. So it was not so bad. Ten days I was in the sanatorium.

I feel quite all right now, and as my baby sleeps quite a lot during the night, (tonight from 10pm till 6.30am!) I am not very tired by her. I am feeding her myself, but since I haven't had sufficiently milk for her I am obliged to give her once a day artificial food. I cook Quaker Oats and she gets half of the Oat water and half of Milk.

She is a good baby but still keeps me busy half the day long. This you know I am sure. How are your children? I have a maid for doing all the washing of linen for us and baby, cooking, and all the hard work. I pay 150 Krowns a month = £1.8 shillings. She is very nice, I am glad.

My sisters now when mother died have a maid who does all the cooking and housework. Gets 180Kč monthly. (£1.12) One sister studies medicine, and the other is eighteen years old and will finish the next year the High Secondary School. I hope to be able to send her next year to England. She knows quite nicely English.

Have heard something that some Guides intend to go to England to camp there in summer next year. (1933) Must ask about it.

I don't run the Company any more since I have got the baby. I have remained only District Captain and Member of the Executive Committee, but have taken now holiday for some months, as I can't now leave baby long when feeding her.

I did not write for some time as I wanted to send a snap of Milena Marie at the same time, and have done the prints only yesterday. I shall be happy to hear from you again, Mrs Campbell. You did not tell me anything about your kiddies. How is Boytzam the dog? I was looking just lately at the snaps from Foxlease and thinking what a lovely time it was.

It is noon, I must go to see what dinner is doing, and to prepare some fruit salad. My husband comes at 12.30 from the office.

Wishing you a very merry Christmas and much happiness in the New Year 1933.

I am yours very sincerely, Anna Rothová

Prague
Dobrovského 4
March 23rd 1933
Dear Mrs Campbell,

Now imagine, that since Xmas I have not answered any Xmas letters from England, isn't it terrible. Nor have I thanked you for any presents, or so. Am quite anxious already to do it. I have got your present and dutifully have opened it at Xmas Eve (which is the greatest moment of the whole Xmas time in our country.) I was thrilled to have got the ruffles or how they are called. They were very useful to me in the coldest time when I was pushing the pram with Milena. They protected perfectly any wisckles.(?)

I have had a busy time all these past months. I am now stopping slowly with feeding the baby, she will be six months on the third of April. I used to feed her cow only once a day, but for all her other meals she gets artificial food. This makes me more free, and I am now going every afternoon to the office with my husband. I have got a very nice maid, she does all the work, and the cooking as well, so I can go out with baby in the morning, and she goes out in the afternoon. In our country we have the flat system mostly, so that we have got no garden and are forced to go for walks with the babies as much as we can into the nearest park. Fortunately I am living very close to a pretty park, so that baby can be out in fresh air very much indeed. She is quite a 'big' baby already, starts trying to sit up, and talks by the international baby language (ug ug ug). She weighs now 6½ kilos.

I must confess that in the first moment I was not quite sure about the ruffles you sent me, what they were for. My husband suggested they might be muffs for baby. But later all the family came for supper, (Xmas Eve they were all my guests), so we determined with my sisters and sister in law that they were ruffles, so used them for this purpose, and they were perfect for this. So I hope we were right.

I know an English family here in Prague and I have got a small Xmas pudding from them. We ate it at Xmas Eve with custard, and everybody liked it.

How are your children? Tell me please some details about them.

My husband was ill end of January and had to undergo an operation. It was not very serious. But still, I was quite frightened you can imagine. My sister who studies medicine has just passed five of her exams, she has now only seven still to pass, and will have her degree. We hope she will do them as well as she has done these. The other sister will just finish the Higher Secondary School, or how you call it, and has now in May and June to pass the last exam with which she can go to the University if she likes to study. I don't know yet if she will study. She is nineteen years old now. She knows English too. I hope to be able to send her this coming summer with a Girl Guide expedition to a camp in England.

Now I want to ask you something. After the camp which will be in July, I should like to leave my sister still for some 3 to 4 weeks in England, as the journey is rather expensive and the fortnight which the Girl Guide expedition plans seems to me rather short. My sister knows well German and fairly well French, so I thought maybe it would be possible to find a family where she could talk with the children German, even French, (but German she knows better),and so she would be able to stay there longer, and know more the English people and English country, and also the English language. I intend to put an advertisement in some Newspaper, but before I do this I am writing you this, as maybe you would know some family who would be interested in this idea. I have not the precise date, but the camp finishes sometime about the 20th July or so. But I shall soon know all the details about place and date, in case you would be interested to know.

We are just painting the walls of one room and the kitchen, so you can imagine how it looks like in the flat. A remarkable mess, all furniture in one room only and my baby like an island in the midst of all this. Baby has a little cold and cough but I hope she will soon be all right again. We have no 'paper painting', we have really and truly the walls painted. A man or two come, take a brush and mix colours in a big pot, make a tremendous mess on the floors and paint the walls at the same time. When they leave everyone is thrilled to see their backs already, and there is still some days afterwards a lot of cleaning and washing to be done, to bring the floors, windows, doors etc to their former state, and furniture, pictures etc their place back again.

I must close as baby must eat now. Butter, flour, milk, water, sugar.
With much love,
yours, Anka

Prague 15th June 1933
Dear Mrs Campbell,

Please pardon that I did not write before. It all was not yet sure and so I did not know what to write. How are you? Is it better now with your kidney? I have been so sorry now to hear about your being ill.

At last now my sister will really go to England but my father was afraid to send her for the first time alone, besides she will have a reduced train fare as well as on the ship they will pay much less, as they (the Czecho-slovak expedition) will join the Belgian and Dutch Girl Guides and so they will get a great reduction. They will visit Bruxelles. Thank you very much for the invitation which I am afraid my sister will be unable to accept. It is a great pity, cannot be done.

Since you were ill you too will want more rest than to take out a guest for sightseeing or so. So maybe it is better when my sister can't accept your invitation. She just has in the next days to pass her last exams in the Higher Secondary School, so she also therefore could not easily leave now. Now I do hope you are not angry with me because she can't accept your invitation! Please say 'No'.

My daughter is a big girl, weighs 9 kilos. She is quite a normal baby now, although she was so small when she was born. She kneels up already, and talks a lot, and altogether she is a happy joyful baby laughing at everything and everybody. Like a good future Brownie! But she hasn't got any teeth yet although eight months old. (she has one, last Monday, 1st July)

My husband is well, thank you.

A great news! We'll remove to a country spot near Prague and shall go by train (35 minutes) to the office. We have hired a country house with big garden with lots of flowers, fruit and vegetables. We shall have there a dog, some white lovely rabbits, (we have bought them already) and other nice things quite new to us and two hens and ten chicks with their mother we have got. Next week we shall move. My maid just is a bit ill so I am fed up. Now when I want her so much to work!

We had an English Girl Guide here in Prague, she learnt German in a German Convent in a frontier town. In Prague she was only to pass her University exam and see all the interesting places.

When you write next time please write to our Prague office address, TRUHLÁŘSKÁ 15, Prague 2.

Yours sincerely, Anka

18th December 1933

Dear Mrs Campbell,

Yours is the first Xmas letter I am writing this year.

What a long time I haven't heard from you, I hope you are well, and also Mr Campbell and your children. I am sending to each of them a 'knife' for opening letters. They are hand painted, and the designs are the real Moravian folk-designs, which can be found on old jugs, plates, etc, still now in the country.

It is also a long time since I wrote for the last time. I hope you know that we live now in the country in a country house. A lovely house though very cold it is here now. You'll be interested to hear some details about how we are freezing here; till the morning water unfreezes in the jug, from 6 a.m. we heat in the kitchen and at 1 p.m. when I wanted a pail which was all the time under the kitchen table, the rest of the last water was still frozen. A sparrow came into our kitchen one day, and found his death by the morning. He was frozen. In the pipes we have no water as the tubes would burst by the frost. I hit eggs out of their shells as they are frozen. The water in the well got frozen, we dont get any water from the pump. So we must go and ask good people in the neighbourhood who still luckily have water to 'borrow' us some. Even to wash nowadays is a luxury. We have 27 degrees under zero Celsius; have it calculated into Fahrenheit and you'll make eyes how we can stand it.

My baby sleeps nevertheless every day outside; 1–2 hours and is quite happy about it, I think. I am enclosing a photo we have enlarged where you'll see Milena how she is stuffed when she goes out. She is a big baby already starts to talk. Says quite plainly 'baby' in English. She has quite a language of herself already.

We hope to go skiing for the Xmas holidays, and intend to put her to her grandmother's, who will be quite grateful to us to have her. She loves Milena quite madly. She weighs about 24 lbs, and has of the fresh air here quite lovely red cheeks.

We must go every day to Prague by train, and I wonder what an opinion we shall have after the winter here, if we shall remain or return to Prague. Although frosts are in Prague too, only that one does not feel winter so hard in town.

And now last not least, Merry Christmas and a Happy New year 1934 to all of you,

much love from Anka Rothová

P.S. My sister was in England and stayed after the Camp with a Reverend in Preston. She liked England very much. I was really sorry you could not see her. I HOPE to get some sound from you Mrs Campbell.

Prague

Truhlářská 15,

Dec 20th 1934

Dear Mrs Campbell,

Again a year has passed. This is to wish you and your family a Merry Christmas and a Happy New Year 1935. Am sending a small purse for your keys. Hope it will be useful to you, and in it one small coin for luck. (our smallest coin, 5 Heller, 0.l of a penny worth!)

My daughter is now two years old. She talks very distinctly and knows her wishes and dislikes. Quite like a person already.

We still are living in the nice house with big garden, and as the winter up to now has been very mild, we have liked it here very much even now in the cold months. Am preserving all the time fruits, and go to the office, and do gardening, rocking my baby, cooking etc etc. Of course we are now in the second winter here and we have arranged everything much better, than the year before. We have learnt from our experience. But the summer here out in the country was delightful. The weather was very dry, not good for vegetables—but a very good weather for fruits. (The Spring was damp). We have 52 fruit trees in our garden, so you may imagine how many fruits we had. I have made jams, jellies, juices. All these things we do ourselves in our country, we don't generally BUY jams and fruit salads. We also pickle eggs, tomatoes, cucumbers, onions, etc. You ought to see my larder, you would be astonished.

We have founded a new Girl Guide Organisation (separated from the Boys association, as it made only difficulties to be with the Boys.) We have started 6 weeks ago, I am in the Committee. We have of course very very much to do, with the start.

Milena was quite all right all the year through, only in Spring she got measles, and angina.[1] She knows words of German, French and English already. She is now like a parrot, everything repeating what she hears.

I am now in the office during the days, which means that Milena is almost always with the maid, and that is the drawback of my living in the country, otherwise everything would be all right.

P.S. I have just wanted to post the letter to you when your present and letter arrived. Oh thank you so much for both, I am thrilled to have got such a nice present and such a long letter.

I must immediately make my letter longer.

I was very interested to hear all the news about the children. How nice that Harry has won a scholarship. I know your schools are very expensive, I felt astonished already when you told me.

We are also very short of drinking water. It seems to be everywhere.

The St Nicholaus brought Milena lovely toys to play with (stove with pots and pans and other utensils for cooking). A dolly, and a toy which I can't describe in English: about seven boxes one in the other, smaller and smaller, and pictures on them. She loves to play with these things. She is all the day with the maid, so she knows how she cooks, washes linen etc and she tries to copy all these works. She also helps already the maid dry up dishes and carries them to the dresser! Like your daughter almost!

For Xmas we shall have a Xmas tree nicely trimmed with all kinds of glittering and sweet things on it.

I am in the office of my father still, but it is no more the office of my father, but the office of my husband, as since $2\frac{1}{2}$ years already, my husband is the owner of the firm, and my father is now active as Manager of a Printing Mill, and Editor of a Magazine. The business is very bad, and we are not much thrilled about it.

One of my sisters, Milada, is a Doctor in the Hospital. Her line is 'Nerves', Psychiatry you know. The other, youngest sister, Zdena, will finish next June her two years course for the Higher School for Social Welfare. She would like to continue in her studies in America—but for this it would be necessary to gain a Scholarship, which of course is not very easy as there are aspirants from all over the world.

I think I have written you quite a lot.

Best wishes to all the family, including Boytsam!

With love, yours sincerely,

Anka Rothová

1. The word "angina" was used to refer to a sore throat at that time.

Leflova 1183

Prague 14

December 19th 1935

Dear Mrs Campbell,

I have been thrilled to have got that nice little apron. Thank you very much indeed.

I too am enclosing a small present, two small covers, or I don't know how you call them, we put them under a vase or so. These small covers, as I call them are both hand made bone-lace and they are much done by the peasants in our country.

As you see from the address we have removed. We are no more living in the country but we have taken a nice flat in Prague again. It is more convenient for us. We have central heating and every comfort that modern living offers, which of course we could not have in the country. Also when I am the whole day in the office, I can easily come home during the midday pause which before was not possible. We are very satisfied with this flat.

I must answer your questions;

I don't think I shall come in the future days to England. I have not the money for such a journey, and I am rather taken up with my household, my duties, my husband, my child, etc.

My sister was in England a year ago and came back quite thrilled. She lived with a pastor family and so could get acquainted with the English life.

I am going every Tuesday to an English Conversation Club, where members are not allowed to talk any other language but English, so I have opportunity to keep up a bit what I know. Of course one still forgets, or better gets out of practice.

As to politics I can't answer you, I must confess I don't understand it.

We have joined the Sanctions, otherwise thank goodness it does not concern us or affect us, if I understand your question.

But talking about politics, I must tell you that our wonderful good President T. G. Masaryk, who was our President since our republic has been declared, resigned of his Presidentship last week. He is very old and he needs rest already. 86 years of great work is very long. Yesterday there took place the vote for the new president, who is now Dr Edvard Beneš, who is well known also abroad as he was our Minister of Foreign Matters and has worked in our League of Nations.[1] We are glad to have Dr Beneš as he was the pupil of Masaryk and to be sure he will be his best successor.

Milena is a big girl, learns German, as I have taken a German maid, so she learns it easily without knowing it even. She learns an English song and says 'Good night' and 'Thank you' in English. She is now 3 years and 2 months old.

You have so big children, time goes quickly, one sees it on the youth.

We shall have a Xmas tree although we are Jews, and don't keep of course religiously the habits of this feast, but it is such a joy for the children to have a Christmas tree and presents under it, so that we also last year trimmed for Milena one. All my family will come on Christmas Eve—which is the greatest feast in our country—for supper.

Merry Chrismas and a Happy and Prosperous New Year 1936 for you and all your family.

Yours with much love

Anka

1. The League of Nations had applied economic sanctions to protest Italy's invasion of Abyssinia (now Ethiopia).

Šimáčkova 22,

Prague 7

December 18th 1936

Dear Mrs Campbell,

Once a year again I must let you hear about me. I have your last letter of 19th January 1935 before me and read how you were pleased to hear I was enjoying living in a flat with central heating etc. As you see from the above address, I had to change once more; the proprietor of the house we lived made suddenly his mind up to marry, and as our flat was the nicest of the house, he chose just our flat to live in it. I should never have expected to be obliged to change the compartment because of an event like this, as he is a gentleman of 55–60 years and was up to that time a bachelor. Imagine! And the wife whom he took was mother of his own nephew's wife, and she divorced of her husband only to be able to marry this old Bachelor. Such tricks plays the life. And I became a victim of this private affair and got notice of my lovely flat and was obliged to remove.

But I am quite satisfied; I have got a flat near to a very big gardens where Milena can be the whole day. I am only about ten minutes walk of my office, so that I do not lose such a lot of time by going to and from the office, and I can live somehow more freely, when I get more time for my child, home, husband and myself. The flat is not so modern as that last one, but as I say, in a way I feel more happy with less comfort and more time, than before with comfort but little time to enjoy it.

I do not know and am a little afraid that I have caused you some bother, as I gave your address to two friends of mine, who both wanted to go to England and were anxious to know a family where they could go as paying guests for the summer. Please excuse me in case it caused any trouble or work.

Milena is a dear. She is 4 years now. Speaks besides Czech rather well German too. I am sending her to a German Kindergarten. We send children to the real school at six years old. I have also a German maid, so it helps a lot when the child has to learn a foreign language. I should like her to know perfectly well German before she goes to school. She of course will go to Czech schools.

I love to read your letters, they always bring something new to me. The children must be very big already. What will be their profession, or is it still too early to think of this? My sisters are, one is Doctor, specialises in nerve diseases, the other one is Social Worker. They both are younger than I am.

I have heard the last speech of your King Edward VIII on the wireless. But I have missed the first speech of H.M. King George VI. It was on a Saturday afternoon and I could not be at home, because I had announced my visit already somewhere.

How is the Boytsam? Is he still alive and in good health? Paní is right for Mrs, which you asked me in your last letter.

My husband is well I am glad to say, but business still is not so good as it ought to be. The unemployment is rather great still in this country, and of course it is felt everywhere, as the capacity of buying of the people gets much smaller, in consequence of this.

I do hope to hear from you again soon. I think this method to write once a year is better than nothing, and I am sure you have forgiven me not to have written sooner. Excuse also my mistakes! I have had last little opportunity for training my English and it is felt already.

Here enclosed a small hand painted with a Slovak design, as book-sign, or how you call it.

Joyous Christmas and a very Happy and Healthy Year 1937.

With much love from Anka

Prague 7
Šimáčkova 22
March 1st 1937

My dear Mrs Campbell,

When I have got your last letter from the 17th January I felt so fed up that you have no idea of it. I felt like if I should be obliged to answer immediately and tell you what happened. It was not quite my fault, you know, and you must be a little patient and let me explain it to you.

When in Spring 1936 my friend wanted for Miss Taussigová some information about a place in England, I said near the countryside I knew only you, and maybe you would know somebody who would take a paying guest for summer, and I gave your address. I must explain that I was quite sure that I was giving the address to a person who was very very all right.

I promise that I shall never give not only yours but any other address to anybody, it is really dangerous. Now I do hope you will forgive me. This was all the consequence of little time and altogether sorrows[1] and so on, which all made full my thoughts, so that I could not have time for smaller things and so have committed mistakes. Once more I am very very sorry, please forgive and do forget it that I was so stupid.

I have not written sooner, because we were all first ill—influenza. First my husband, then I, then Milena, then the maid twice, and I was ill for a fortnight. Then I got a sort of dizziness and felt like sea sick all the time. But it is better today again.

My husband goes next week abroad, to Egypt and Palestine, commercially, so I shall be a very long time alone. I shall feel lonely, I know. But for him it is lovely. He was born in Alexandria and was brought up there. He has been in Czechoslovakia only 17 years. Since that time this will be for the first time when he'll come to his native land. I am glad for him. Milena is all right again, but still a little pale. We need Spring already.

How marvellous that you know some Czech. You ought to come to Czechoslovakia to be able to practice your knowledge or you'll forget it! Thanks so much for the snap of your country house. How nice to hear that you remember my love for thatched roofs! It is lovely to have such a house in the country. I am already reflecting where to put my little daughter for the summer months. I want to hire some room, (a room and kitchen) near Prague so that I can often come out and be there too with her.

When I have a snap of me and Milena I shall send it to you. You see I lived two years in such a whirl that I had not time to enjoy my life. But now it starts to be much better again.

I shall be ever so glad when I shall hear from you again soon, and when you will tell me you have forgiven me for giving your address.

With love, yours very sincerely,

Anka

1. The sorrows she refers to must, I think, have been a combination of bad business

conditions and the ominous situation developing in Europe after Hitler's accession to power in 1933.

Mildred was another Guide friend, to whom my mother wrote most warmly and from the heart. Although we never met, she, like several of my mother's other friends, wrote me kind letters and sent presents during my childhood in England.

The unhappiness referred to in the following letter is probably related to Hitler's drastic acts in Europe: his absorption of Austria in March, followed by the Munich agreement signed by Britain, France, and Italy in September, which allowed Germany to annex Sudetenland, in northwestern Czechoslovakia. The Czechs thus in effect lost much of their homeland.

This is the first crisis time I remember, my chief impression being of extra supplies, lamps and food, being stored against some nameless emergency. My parents listened anxiously to the radio.

Šimáčková 22
Prague 7
December 18th 1938
Dear Mildred,

This is just to tell you my best thanks for your nice and comforting words, which just arrived in the time when all our hearts were literally bleeding.

It is now quiet here, but things have got a new feature. A funny thing. The same object, and it has changed its feature, the same man and he has changed his view to look at things. It would be interesting if it weren't so tragical, as I said already once today in a letter.

But I do hope for the Czechoslovak nation that there will come again sun and happiness.

We are all well, my daughter looking forward with great anxiety to Xmas and all the presents she will have under her Xmas tree. I have started to teach her English but I was so busy the past two months that I had to stop.

How are you always, Mildred. It was so nice to read your letter.

Please accept my heartiest wishes for a Merry Xmas and a very happy New Year 1939.

With love, yours sincerely, Anka

P.S. Heda sends her love too, so does Marjánka. My younger sister will get married in January. These are all the news here.

Only somehow the sun is always behind the clouds, and this gives the life such a grey colour. It is the lot of unhappiness that is seen around us.

Šimáčkova 22,

Prague 7

December 18th 1938

Dear Mrs Campbell,

From day to day I have postponed to answer your dear and precious letter, but as always without any result. I have been since 18th October, that means just 2 months so busy, that I had to work more than 3 weeks at home till 12 or 1 at night. All only work for the office. I felt almost ill of it, because I cannot well do night work. I am a good sleeper and if I have not sufficient sleep I cannot work at daytime. My gall is not very bad, but not quite in order, but it is a little my fault, as I am not quite keeping to the right diet. The diet is not so very severe, so I ought to keep to it. But I am too busy to think of me and that is that.

Thank you very much indeed for your kind words. I do hope that the time will not be so bad that I should be ever forced to use your offer; one never knows, the experiences of the past year have given us a very good lesson so that we count with every possibility. Maybe that you still remember my being of Jewish confession which is a chapter for itself in Central Europe.

Besides that by the changement of the frontier of the village that my husband's family belonged to, is now in Hungary, so we wonder what will happen with our nationality, or citizenship. I was born in Prague, our family was always a Czech family, I was in Czech schools, my husband has been living in Prague since 1920, so I hope that this will help, that we shall be able to vote for Czechoslovakia, and will not become Hungarian citizens. We should not be an exception, as this happened to thousands of families, that from one day to the other, they have become German, Polish or Hungarian citizens.

My friend's mother and sister were obliged to leave Carlsbad where they lived for 40 years, within 24 hours, and they came to my friend; but as Sudeten refugees they will not be allowed to remain here. Where can they go? And such cases we see round about us every day. We are sad in our minds, we cannot help, we only are thoughtful about all that happens and what still can happen.

If I should be still an unmarried girl, I should go to England and I am sure that I could make myself useful. But with a family I am not at all sure that England would be the right place. Maybe it will quiet down, but just now there is a wave here to emigrate. There are thousands of people who are forced to emigrate, who cannot remain here, all former Czechoslovak citizens. I have relatives who must emigrate, because they have no other choice. In case you would have in some Colonies or Dominions some friends or relatives, could you not give me their address and I should try to ask them for informations about the possibility of immigration to those places? Thanks very much indeed.

If it would be possible and things would be a bit normal I should very much like to go to England in Summer, but I do not dare to make any plans yet.

Oh, just arrived your Xmas card and the lovely small cover. Thank you very much indeed. I too am enclosing today a small, wee gift for you; a collar. I have bought it for you in Carlsbad—it belongs now to Germany. I was there last Spring. The people work laces and such things in the villages there.

Your little cover I shall use for the first time on Xmas Eve when I shall have here a great party again. My youngest sister will marry in January and so the party this time will be extraordinary festival like.

I shall be very glad when you will have time to write to me some news about you and your family.

With kindest regards and remembrances,

Yours very sincerely,

Anka

Germany invaded Czechoslovakia on March 15, 1939, just two days before my mother wrote the following letter. The persecution of the Jews was already well advanced in Germany, and it was now urgent to flee.

Šimáčkova 22,
Prague 7
17th March 1939
My dear Mrs Campbell,

After the recent changes in the last days you most probably have thought of your friend in Prague. Well I must send a few lines to you. We all are in good health and in order. Your last letter has made me a great joy, but up to today I have written neither to New Zealand nor Canada. From New Zealand my friends have got negative answer because they let very small numbers in. From Canada the answers are all very doubtful. Only farmers can get in. But I have decided to write to both addresses in the following days.

The purpose of my letter today is to ask you if you could find a post for me in England as a cook so that I could get permit for coming there and work there. I have written in this manner to another friend in England too. I have just looked into the form where all the conditions are under which people can enter England. I shall copy it for your information and enclose it with this letter. I think for me as married woman, two comes into consideration. For the married couple, she as cook and domestic worker, he as gardener, chauffeur, and other work in the same family. If you would know about such a post we should accept it with my husband. We should then see what could be done with our little daughter. Once already when the mobilisation came my friend wrote me that I may put Milena to her and her mother. She is a teacher. Maybe it would do. You too were so kind to give me your proposals, but owing to the fact that I have no money abroad, and in the last few months the National Bank here has not allowed any money, or very limited money, for abroad, I cannot only come and live there and wait until I get possibility to go overseas, but I must work and be able to live of it. Besides without a permit for work I shall not get the permission to enter England.

Please get in touch with my friend,[1] because it will be quicker than to write to me, and maybe one of you will have the possibility to find a post like that for me and my husband, and then apply for the permit to the Home Office. Our dates are;

Anna Rothová, née Steinová, born in Prague on the 24th November 1905.

My husband, Emil Roth, born in Alexandria Egypt on 10th November 1902.

My daughter, Milena Marie, born in Prague 3rd October 1932.

Besides that, maybe you will not be able to find a post for me, but owing to the fact that your husband is a doctor, maybe you would easier know about a post for my sister. She is a Doctor, specialist for nervous and mental diseases, or as nurse for a person who needs to have somebody. As hospital nurse, you can see as to the enclosed form, she could get a permit for entering and working in England too.

Her dates, Milada Steinová, M.D.Prague 2, Soukeniska 29, born on 8th Feb 1908 in Prague.

I do hope you will understand this letter of mine and that it will be possible for you to do something in this matter.

Looking forward to an answer of yours,

Yours very sincerely,

Anka Rothová

1. The friend she mentions is another Girl Guide, Elsie, who took a very active part in our attempted rescue and, later, in my life.

Prague

March 21st 1939

I think I have given you the wrong month of my husband's birth. It is 10th November on his passport.

I have just heard of a cousin of my friend who has got a post in a home for children. (I don't know how you call such a home in England) and she has been able to take her child there too and does the cooking. This wouldn't be bad for me. I should do any work for the children or in the house.

I shall be glad when I shall hear from you. The first day in Spring but it freezes and snows like in January.

I hope you are all doing well. In these days I somehow seem to have forgotten all my English.

With love,
yours very sincerely,
Anka

I don't remember how old I was when Doris handed me all these letters and papers; I think I was well under twenty. She'd never hidden them, and I'd read them from time to time over the years, always finding something new. Mostly I would be trying to recapture my mother's personality and get closer to that time when I had actually been her daughter. I remember being impressed by her mildly philosophical comment "Such tricks plays the life" about our being turned out of our home because of the landlord's unexpected marriage. Though far from profound, her comment showed an attitude that was very different from the heavily concrete thinking in my new milieu, her patient acceptance of life's discomforts contrasting with the indignant ranting and raving with which, I later discovered, Doris would greet the smallest inconvenience.

Among all these papers, Doris had marked one envelope "miscellaneous"; it contained brief letters, bearing aristocratic names and addresses, from rather grand people in England to whom she had also appealed for help in the rescue of my family. All were benevolent if not actively helpful, and the letters show to her very great credit how hard she worked to save us. But among them are two whose significance I've been slow to grasp, perhaps because they express attitudes that I've been brought up with and took so much for granted myself. They throw into sudden relief the atmosphere in Prague and the world at that time.

These letters are from the non-Jewish parents of a girl named Ela, who was at boarding school with the Campbells' youngest child, Jane. The two were friends, and Ela had obviously been a guest of the Campbells during part of her summer holidays.

The first is innocuous, handwritten by Ela's mother a few years earlier.

Prague 7

September 29th 1936

Dear Mrs Campbell,

I was so pleased to get your note, especially as I was just going to write myself to thank you for everything you are doing for Ela. It certainly is most kind of you to come to the rescue so promptly and I can never thank you enough for having accepted Ela into your home. She is so happy with you and Jane, and she thinks nature is great for having arranged an epidemic at the right moment to give her a chance to enjoy such a lovely holiday with you. I only hope she is not giving you too much trouble with her colds and things. Why, she has even been borrowing handkerchiefs from you, and there are 30 new handkerchiefs marked with her name, sent to the school from London! I don't know what you will think of the poor child, let loose on the world with 5 handkerchiefs. . . . [1]

Yours sincerely,

H.T.

1. And on she goes with her thanks.

Despite H.T.'s glowing gratitude for Doris's hospitality, I found that Doris spoke of Ela for years with the jeering disapproval she felt toward most people, not only foreigners. I heard stories of what a spoiled and obnoxious child Ela had been, how rich, lazy, and ungrateful. She even threw away her stockings if they had holes and runs in them instead of mending them, and she always wanted her own way in everything!

In 1939 however, there is a typewritten letter from Ela's father, in response to a request from Doris for help in speeding our escape. Czechoslovakia had been under occupying German control for ten days when he wrote the following letter.

25.3.39

Dear Mrs Campbell,

I am afraid I can be of no help to your friend here in Prague, as no visas or entrance permits are given by the Prague office without a Home Office permit, which must be obtained direct in London. . . . [1]

Whilst I fully appreciate your kindness and generosity in trying to help your Jewish friend, I should advise you not to get unduly worried: the Jews here are no worth [*sic*] off then the rest of the nation. There is no Jew baiting and not likely to be. Of course they are not a very brave race, and it's them who come squealing to the Legation, and they all want to leave the country. Those people who are in real danger, such as former Czech political leaders etc, and the rest of the nation, set their teeth and will have to bear it somehow. But apparently, to get sympathy nowadays you must be a Jew. The Czech Jews in particular are in no danger whatsoever—but of course there were not many Czech Jews in this country; most of them have always been disloyal to the Republic and proclaimed themselves as Germans and carried out germanisation in every big town; it's those latter of course who come under the more stricter laws.

I do not think you will be doing your country a very good service in the long run in taking all these people in. It's true they offer now to go to domestic service and work, but they won't stay there long; at least it has been our experience in Central Europe that they, as the richest and most influential race in the world, never do any manual work, but soon obtain control of commerce, finance, and all the more profitable trades.

Helping one or two persons is like trying to clear up the slums of London by dropping a penny into a hat; I really think personally, and my opinion is shared by many, that the whole question will have to be solved radically, and that some portion of land will have to be given to them somewhere in the world, where at last they can live as a nation, among themselves, occupying all positions, being servants and road sweepers and smiths and everything, and not only businessmen and bankers. Please do not think me unsympathetic, I certainly do not approve of persecution in any form, and the brutal manner in which some policies are at present enforced in some parts of the world.

But I do think the Jews have had a very good run for their money in this part of the world, and even if they have to give up some of their money, (and they all have plenty of it here I assure you), it's not so hard as the national humiliation inflicted on the nation as a whole, which they do not feel, as they have only their personal interest and suffering in view.

Our future is very uncertain, and we can only hope that things will settle down a bit soon to normal, as these upheavals are most nerve wracking; and that we shall be able to live and work in peace, if we prove goodwill and loyalty to our new masters. After all, here we have been for twenty years loyal to France who left us in the lurch at the time of the Munich agreement, which allowed Czechoslovakia to be invaded.

My daughter is still at boarding school in England as you know, and I have to thank you for all the kindness you have ever showed her. She certainly appreciated it, especially the trips to your country cottage. I expect she will have to come back here, to what God only knows. My job I expect will go west soon, and not being Jews, we have little hope of finding benefactors or refuge in your beautiful country.

With kind regards,

yours sincerely,

I.T.

1. To summarize the rest of this paragraph, he puts responsibility squarely on the heads of the guarantors in England.

Doris did not share the views of Ela's father, at least to my knowledge, and I never heard him mentioned.

Prague

10th April 1939

Dear Mrs Campbell,

I was so happy on Saturday when at noon I found your letter about Míla in the post. She of course was immediately for accepting it and has already written to Dr Martin that she wants to accept. This letter had not been posted when already another letter arrived, that the Guides headquarters have written about a post with a mental patient. I quickly rang up Míla to ask her whether she perhaps would rather like this post.

I also feel quite muddled, and do not know what I have written any more and what not, because the days are so full. I have today the housedressmaker at home, and there is a Bank Holiday so that I was all the day helping with sewing. All frocks of Milena must be made longer and all together she must also get a few new things. She will not know a great lot of English, but it will not seem quite foreign for her at least in the beginning. She had 2 weeks holiday from school; tomorrow she will have for the first time school again. Our school year begins in September and finishes in June.

My maid has also two and a half days holidays, but it is almost midnight and she said she would return at 8pm and she is not yet here. She left the keys here, so I must now wait for her. I feel quite tired already.

My youngest sister, who married in February has arrived in London last Tuesday. It was so exciting before she left and also her voyage was interesting.

Yesterday we were in Hloubětín for the whole day, it is a suburb of Prague, where my husband's mother lives. She is very ill with the heart, and has suffered lately very much. She lives with Lisa, the sister of my husband. My husband was gardening the whole day and I have done some cooking, to have a bit of practice. Mrs Mathewson has written me a very nice letter, and I am just writing to her too. I do hope she will be satisfied with me, and before I get accustomed to the country, I can just as well, for a week or two, work for a smaller wage or for nothing. I shall be happy to find a home, and am no 'grand lady' who would be afraid of work or consider one work better than the other.

I am glad that you are looking forward to see Milena and I do hope it will not mean too great a work for you to have her there. Elsie also writes that she can have her there for the term, so I do hope that for the beginning it will do, and then let us hope it will somehow develop.

With much love yours as ever, Anka

In none of her letters did my mother make explicit at what point she finally decided we must all leave. By the time of the April 10 letter, above, the decision was a fait accompli, and she still had hope that we would be traveling together. She also did not make clear at what point she heard of the possibility of children leaving by train, unaccompanied by parents—the Kindertransport.

Only when I read the correspondence between Doris and Elsie in England did I realize that my father had not given permission for me to travel alone until June 1939, just a month before I left. By that time, the trains to take children out alone had been organized and were moving.

My mother's next letter, another to her friend Mildred, is mostly concerned with mutual friends who are not part of this story. The relevant part is reproduced below.

Prague,
1st May 1939
Dear Mildred,

Milena is learning English, but I am so busy, that I cannot teach her and learn with her at home, so I am afraid, it is very slow and she will not learn very much. But she is quick with languages, so I hope she will quickly learn it later, when she needs it.

I really shall be very glad to see you again. I hope that matters will go on nicely. My work permit application was accepted here, so I do hope that also this matter will be all right, as first I was told that as a married woman, I must apply with my husband together, as a married couple. Let us hope that my application will not come back without result, because of this reason. But there are always exceptions, so I hope that I shall be one of the exceptions—or that meanwhile will appear a post for a married couple. We shall see. You see it was so funny. Everyone whose turn was before me and was married and had a new application, was told to come after the 1st May, or to come with the husband and was sent home again. And all at once when my turn came, and I was already prepared to hear a negative answer, the lady said, 'Let us accept just a few' and she took my application, with all documents, photos, etc. She did not ask if I were married, nothing whatsoever. It was marvellous.

We have been today in Rez for the whole day. That is the place where we lived for two years in the country. Everything is just in blossom, it was a lovely day. Milena met all her old friends, she felt very happy.

Dear Mildred, please accept my great thanks for your kindness and tell to all our friends my best regards. They must excuse me if I dont write to everyone often. I simply cannot. It is not possible. I think I shall do it now in turns.

With love,
yours very sincerely,
Anka

Prague
4th May 1939
Dear Mrs Campbell,

It is a very long time since I have heard from you or you from me. Or it seems only for me such a long time, I do not know. Time passes, every day brings something new. And always interesting. I have succeeded to hand over the green form which Mrs Mathewson signed with a lot of necessary documents to Miss Wellington, the lady who is here having her office of the Central Bureau of Refugees.

This is a marvel that I have succeeded in this and it would be a very long story if I should relate you all about it. She was not allowed to take new applications for some time, and says that I cannot count to get the permit before 8 weeks. She has accepted my application for 26th April. This was quite an exceptional case, because she was allowed to accept new applications not before the 2nd May, and I have heard from a young girl, a friend of mine, who had to hand over her application today, that again no applications have been accepted today. So mine is there and let us hope has gone already to England. If so we can count according to Miss Wellington that at the end of June the Permit would arrive. Perhaps I shall get in the meantime the Guarantor's Permit (also yours for Milena) for which was sent the application to London by Elsie on 29th March. But Miss Wellington says if it were possible for me to wait for the work permit here, it would be better for me, because she says if I go on a Guarantor permit to England it is more difficult to get the work permit there than to get it here.

So we shall see how matters will develop. Do you think I have to write to Mrs Mathewson? Could she wait till the end of June? Because she wrote on the 5th April, that she could wait 8 weeks, which was understood to the 5th June. It would be good if she knew how matters stand, do you not think? But as I do not like to spoil something, I am awaiting your advice.

As to my sister; she has written to the Gentleman in Salisbury, and he has written that he is willing to wait 6 weeks for her and hold the post open for her. She was to see a Miss Wilson, who has her office for the nurses only, and she told her that she can accept her and her application on the 13th May, not before, because she has booked 30 other applicants before my sister. Since that date at least 8 weeks, one must again count for the Permit, before it comes.

My sister is quite unhappy, and distressed if the Gentleman cannot wait for such a time. She has tried every possible way. She came to see me last night and asked me to write you and ask you to be kind enough and write to the gentleman in Salisbury if he would not mind if she would get the Permit later, because the lady said that by no means can a Permit be here before eight weeks, and she has to tell that to the employer. My sister thinks that if she would write maybe he would lose his patience, but if you tell him, maybe he will wait longer, until the Permit would arrive. Of course there is running also the guarantor Permit for my sister, if it would arrive sooner, or if she could work before it comes. I have heard they sometimes take only 4–5 weeks. This is a grave question.

We are all all right. I have got a defense [prohibition] of work here, so there is an end of my work here. I only tremble what will come with Emil. Milena is learning a little English, not very quickly, she has the lessons only once a week. I have not found a better course for children. But I think later she will be quick with the learning of it. I am visiting a course for cooking so that I know some new things. It is very interesting.

I shall be glad to hear news of all your family,

Yours with much love,

Anka

A chicken-and-egg situation had developed, in which people without jobs could not get an exit permit, while those with job offers stood to lose the job because the permits were so slow in being granted.

My mother underplays the loss of her job, but it was a disaster, the beginning of the end, and the penultimate step to my parents' being dispossessed altogether. They relied on their joint work to support them. I did learn lately, however, that she also had the job of managing the block of flats they lived in, collecting the rents, etc., and lived there rent-free. I don't know how long this lasted.

The first part of the following letter is filled with more administrative details about all the places she has been to and her attempts to persuade people to hurry her application, and she wonders if Mrs. Mathewson could claim that she needs Anka's help very urgently. She has also discovered that the Midlands Girl Guide Committee applied directly for a permit for one of her friends, which came through in two weeks, and wonders if the same could be done for her sister Míla.

Prague,
13th May 1939
Dear Mrs Campbell,

I have written to Mrs Mathewson and informed her about the permit and also asked her to be so kind to wait for me a bit longer. Let us hope that it really will not take longer than 8 weeks.

As to Míla now. Imagine, she again was not accepted. Queues and queues are waiting and only always an exception is admitted, and if admitted it does not yet mean that the papers will be accepted. The people (of the Refugee Committee) are overburdened.

It does not matter, as matters stand, just now, if I leave in June. For me it does not matter, but it matters only if Mrs Mathewson would not be able to wait. Then of course it would matter awfully.

Only with my husband I have great sorrows. Would you by any chance know of some kind of post in business or factory. But I am afraid if it would help him, as who knows if then he would get a permit for such a sort of job. I am afraid that not. I really have no idea up to now what to do with him.

It is raining in torrents the whole day. I have been at home all the time, it simply was not possible for me to get out. Just now it has stopped so I shall go to post all my letters that I have written today.

I do hope to hear again some lines from you. The situation is not at all sunny. Thank you for everything. Milena sends her love. She knows all her Aunts in England by name.

With much love and kindest regards from my husband,
Yours very sincerely,
Anka

Although it may seem a little strange that my mother and not my father took the initiative in all these matters, I suppose that he was in effect a foreigner in Czechoslovakia. His Czech was not perfect, and he'd actually lived there only seventeen years, whereas Prague was her lifelong home town, she knew how to get around the system, and she had all the contacts in England. Whether she had more foresight and initiative than he had, I just don't know.

I also don't know if his business trip to Egypt and Palestine had anything to do with attempts to escape, but I never heard anything to that effect, and in fact other letters that I've recently seen show that he did some selling there for his firm.

Although I was present at this time, I remember only the hushed discussions of the elders. But that in itself is a very horrible memory.

Prague
23rd June 1939
Dear Mrs Campbell,

I have sent you on the 8th June a Medical Certificate for Milena, and her 2 photos, as I was told to send them to you, because the Central Committee for Refugees (Children's Department) would require them, and if these documents arrive in time, that it would be possible that Milena goes with the next transport of children. (Either end of June or 15th July) Now since that time I have got no news from you whether you have got the Medical Certificate and the photos. If not please write by return if I should send them once more. The next transport goes (as I have enquired here,) on the 28th June, so if it arrives for her it can be only for the 15th July, because amongst these children chosen for the 28th June, she is not.

The date of 15th July seems to me very favourable, because she would just have time to get a little accustomed to the language before she gets to school, don't you think so? I have overcome already also the first sad feeling, and hope that we shall meet soon again. My husband is in the country since Thursday last.

So if Milena goes too and my permit does not arrive soon I shall be here alone. But some of my friends who have applied some short time before me, have got the Permit in the last days, so I may hope that mine will arrive soon too.

With Míla the situation has not yet changed. I am afraid she will lose at last that job in Salisbury. But we shall see. Perhaps it gets a turn to another side soon. If nothing comes (I mean my Permit) to the end of June, I shall go to urge it to Miss Wellington here. She told me not to come until she would write me. But I shall dare it nevertheless and notwithstanding.

It's just 4.15 AM! I have got up a little too early. The thoughts don't leave me sleep. Please write if you have got the photos and Certificate, and if you have sent them to Bloomsbury House.[1]

How are you, your children and your husband? Perhaps you could tell me some news in your next letter? Milena has her last day at school today, or better she just goes to school to fetch her certificate.

Our school term begins then on 1st September. More than 2 months holidays our children get. When does a school year begin in England? Milena has just started to look up words in the dictionary, in case she would want something urgently, (like handkerchief, she says) Otherwise she'll talk by means of her hands. She is not at all bothered about this and looks forward to the journey. I am glad about this.

Kindest regards,
yours very sincerely,
Anka

1. Bloomsbury House was the center in London where all refugee matters were processed.

The next letter, dated July 3, 1939, is the last I have of those written before my departure for England on, I think, July 18. My mother was obviously getting ready to send me ahead of herself and my father. Her job with Mrs. Mathewson must have fallen through because of the delay, and Doris had offered both my mother and father jobs in her house, as receptionist for her husband's medical office and gardener-chauffeur for the household.

My mother sees this as lifesaving, and the letter overflows with gratitude. This letter shows that things have become desperate, and she is preparing me for the move. I think Doris had actually lost the domestic couple who normally lived downstairs and did this work—she lost all her servants, either to factories or to the armed forces, soon after war started—so the opportunity to employ my parents suited her, too.

Although I knew I was escaping with my life, I don't remember feeling afraid, which is strange, as I remember many other fears.

I clearly remember us packing two suitcases together. My mother filled one with all the family linens—many that she must have had made before she was married, for they were embroidered with her maiden initials, A.S.—and the lace tablecloths made by her mother. She also packed the dark-red silk with the cream-colored bird and my hand-embroidered Czech peasant outfit in dark lovely colors, with its many petticoats, puffed sleeves, and richly embroidered apron and headband. There was a doll in a matching outfit. Last but not least, she included her two diaries, written in Czech, which she had started when I was born, describing every bit of my progress until I was four. My own suitcase was filled with clothes, books, toys. I can see us both bent over the suitcases on the floor at the dining end of our living room. We are discussing what I should take. I see myself moving my arms and talking, but I don't know what I said. I know I was left with the uneasy feeling that I had somehow made the wrong choices. As to what I felt, it's a blank. I see myself like a moving doll who is dumb but wants to speak.

The cases were marked with an identifying exit number in huge figures, in heavy green paint roughly applied. It is one of these I kept safely, realizing it was a historic object, until last year, when I heard that the new Holocaust Exhibition of the Imperial War Museum in London, opening in the summer of 2000, was looking for artifacts. This suitcase had followed me around the world, up and down to attics and basements, across to North America and back again to England; it was amazing that it still existed, for it could only be used for storage, as its handle had gone. But I knew I couldn't take it with me to the next life, nor cut it into three for my children, so here was a perfect chance to give it a good home.

I phoned the museum in the early days of its planning, and spoke to the man in charge of collecting artifacts. He had just come out of a meeting with his boss, who had said, "We must have a suitcase." He couldn't believe the offer I was making. Sixty years had passed since the case was packed. So now the suitcase, the doll—hairless, but still in her peasant skirt—and the last photo taken of our family are displayed in the new museum, and copies of these letters from my mother are in its archives.

She put a list of instructions for Doris inside the case. One was the comment that my boots would all need reheeling. I can remember actually seeing the old Czech cobbler mending them himself on the counter in the doorway of his hole-in-the-wall workshop, and banging tiny wooden pegs into the leather soles. Doris had practical sense and could see that they were all newly repaired, and took them to her own local cobbler, who removed the heels, to find all my mother's jewelry inside. I felt proud to be a smuggler at six and a half, but it does now seem an extreme risk to have taken. Perhaps she thought her need for money would be desperate.

In her letter of May 4, 1939, and in the following one, she mentions the prohibition of her work, which clearly was no longer in her own or her father's office. All Jewish businesses were probably closed by now, and I don't know what had happened to Grandfather's work either.

Šimáčkova 22
Prague 7
July 3rd 1939
Dear Mrs Campbell,

I have had both your letters, of the 26th and 29th June. I feel awfully grateful, and excited. This you can immagine [*sic*]. And please tell your husband, that we both my husband and I, thank for your great kindness. I feel perfectly sure Milena will be safe in your hands and it is really for the moment the best for her. Let us hope that it will not take a too long time and that we all three, Milena, my husband and I can soon live together as it was before. When I read your letter I cried over the great kindness of yours. You as mother will make yourself an idea what I feel about sending away Milena, but I try to make myself persuaded that it is the right way we do in sending her away and really the time is not for sentimental feelings. She herself is looking forward to it and I have bought also today the

Dictionary. I shall send it to you next Tuesday or Wednesday, because I want first to show it to Milena how to find words in it.

She is for this week with her Grandmother [my father's mother] in Hloubětín, a suburb of Prague, and I shall fetch her on Sunday home again. She is still a small child and does not understand what this sending her away means. Just yesterday I related to her about the hot water bottle you gave in your house into my bed and how it made me terribly afraid when I jumped into the bed. She laughed loudly when I related it to her.

She is a very good child with very much good will, and she always tries to do so as it is right. But of course as with all children one must know the right way to treat her. She can dress and undress herself, brush her teeth and wash herself. She is a very good eater and eats everything. She does not like fish. She loves milk. Raw fruit and raw carrots etc she is very much fond of. If you still would like something that would be good to teach her, please tell it to me.

She gets up at seven or half passed seven and eats a small breakfast, as it is usual in this country, just coffee and a roll. We have no big breakfast as it is the custom in England. But at ten o'clock we eat the second 'breakfast', bread and butter, bread and jam etc. At noon we have the biggest meal with meat, soup etc. At four p.m. we drink coffee and bread and butter. She only eats bread and butter or a cake, fruit or whatsoever, not much, and at seven p.m. we eat the supper.

Her supper consists of bread and butter and milk, or bread and butter and an egg, boiled or fried, or some ham, and so on. I do not think she will much like porridge in the beginning, but I hope she will get accustomed to it, as it was the case with me. I love porridge now. I think it will be easy to accustom her to the English time of meals and to the English food. When she will see the others to eat like that, she will like to do it as the others do it. But maybe in the beginning she would be hungry if she would get the last meal at 4.30 p.m. Although I know your tea is such a big meal that it would be perfectly sufficient. This will show the experience.

I want to send also Czech books with her things, Fairy Tales etc. because I should like her to have something of her own language near her and not to feel quite lonely. And then I should not like her to forget quite the mother tongue. Children are very quick about this. She said to me not long ago: 'In the beginning I shall write to you in Czech.' She means to write me later in English. But it really would be a pity if the child would forget her own language. If I should be lucky and the Permit of mine arrives soon, then of course all this gets another feature.

I think Zdena could fetch her in London, because as you know, she, my sister, is in London. It would be very good if she herself could bring the child to your home. How much does it cost, the journey, London to you, return ticket? I should ask Zdena if she could afford it. I think the beginning for Milena would be easier if her Auntie Zdena would bring her to her new home. The word 'Mummy' sounds so much like the Czech 'mami' that in the first moment when I read your letter I felt quite repentant. And I immediately thought it would not make me so sad if she said Auntie to you. But maybe that if your children would call you like that she would like it too. Please do as you think best. I am sure you will find the right way.

VITÁME TĚ MILENO—we welcome you Milena. When we call or address somebody, the termination 'O' means we call to her like that or we are speaking to her.

I understand every word you said about Elsie, but when you will see her I am sure you will like her. And she means it also as best as she can, but is overstrained and maybe that is why the way of her telling things was not so as you would like it. I told her once, in the beginning in March, already, in one letter, that she has to join all the threads together, because it was impossible for me to reply to all my friends separately. It was necessary that in the hands of one person concentrates the whole matter. And as I know Elsie longer and most of all, and she also was here in Prague and knows me and my family personally, I thought I could not trouble you more than I did and wrote her to join the threads in her hands. And that is maybe why she feels responsible for the whole matter. Do you understand? She is very good and very nice, and if there would be something you would not like, please tell me. I am sure, it will be all right. Of course I shall not tell her about what you have written to me.

Milena will have sufficient dresses I think for this and the coming year, because all the things have been made long and can be made still longer. When she leaves and when I send all her things, I shall write you a special list, so that you know particulars about everything.

I am now alone at home as the child is at Grandmother's and my husband is working in the country, as I told you I think. I have worked until Saturday still in the office. On Friday evening my principal all at once stopped my work. So it is now really finished.

I had visitors in the house, some people who left for Italy on Friday. A mother with two daughters. A great excitement in the house with them and their affair. Not quite simple. But all is well that ends well, so this also ended well.

But it made it quite impossible to write or do anything else.

Just when they left, some two hours after that, my principal told me that it was my last day of work. I had only a small contract since April, which could be stopped every day. The day arrived. I cried the whole evening on Friday. Then I prepared all the things for the child and took her to the Grandmother and returned last night at 10 p.m.

So I am now at home and have the time to prepare all the things for Milena. She will have a new coat for winter and a Mackintosh [raincoat]. Have I to buy her Wellingtons, I mean such high rubber boots? Our children do not wear them much, but they are to be had here too. I remember when I was in England all the children wore these boots. If you still have an idea about what she ought to have I should be grateful for every wink.

I have given notice to my maid because as I do not work now, and with my husband's reduced income, I must be very careful. It is very good for me now, because I shall be forced to do some housework. It will be good training for me.

As for Míla, the matter well may be change. We shall see, I shall still tell you.

One does not know what the next day brings.

I shall go on Friday to the Children's Committee to make enquiries. I was not yet there, because first I thought the child would go with me.

Now I shall ask about the luggage the children are allowed to have and when the next batch of children will go, etc.

The way of educating our children is maybe a little different to yours, so please I think in the beginning you will be, may be, obliged to be a little patient with our Milena. But as she really is very adaptable, I do hope, she will find out, and feel out what you require from her. She will come to a new milieu and the new habits will just belong to it and she will think that it is not otherwise possible and will forget her old way of doing things.

How are you? I was quite alarmed that you do not feel well and that you will be obliged to undergo an operation in Autumn. My gallstones are very nice and I can eat everything, so I am very glad. Now when I am not in the office, I do hope to get a little stronger again. I need it awfully. I have slept so little, that yesterday I took some pills that Míla gave me and so I hope now that it will be all right. Tonight it was after a long time the first night when I slept it through.

I hope you will excuse all my mistakes. The principal thing is when you can understand what I mean.

Tomorrow I have a needle woman in the house, we shall sew different things for Milena. Some nighties, and the chemises, I hope it is said like that. Also two aprons. Do children wear aprons in your country. Here they are not allowed to come to school without apron. But they may each have a different apron, not all the same.

It is half passed ten, I must go to bed.

Kindest regards,

Anka

I had already left, before this next letter. There is no letter describing the preparations or departure; or, if there was, it was not preserved. I'm very grateful to Doris for respecting my mother enough to keep all these letters and give them to me.

The trains left late at night. I can remember the scene clearly. It was a huge, dark, cavernous station, with high arched ceilings, lit by glaring whitish lights, rather threatening. All the parents jammed the station to see their children off. We all wore labels, and I remember distinctly that my feeling of refugeedom began with the label. There was a dead silence. All my family was present, so my cousin Eva Roden says in her memoir. She claims that I screamed for my mother, but I have no recollection of that at all. I was excited, and I remember sitting in a corner seat next to the window on the right, swinging my legs and looking out at all the people on the platform. There were about eight children in our carriage, and that is all I can recall about our departure. Yet somehow I can *smell* it. I do remember that, after a while, tiredness and reality took over, and it ceased to be fun.

We were aware of reaching the Dutch border. Holland had not yet been invaded by Germany, and the atmosphere changed. I didn't know it at the time, but from that moment we were free. The train stopped, and we all got out. We had a picnic in a field, on the grass. The boys kicked a football, and the girls sat around on the ground. I remember the high wire-mesh fence around the field. And then the train took us on until we arrived at Hook of Holland, where a large boat awaited us. I can remember that the lower bunk, which I was given to sleep in, had very nice clean white sheets. After we arrived in England, we got on another train, which took us to London.

There was a big hall—I know now that it was at Liverpool Street Station, in the financial heart of the city; it's as clear as today. I waited in this hall, which seemed to have a high roof and cream paint but was dirty. There was a crowd of children, and I was at the very back. I had a small peaked straw hat with red, white, and blue tassels which I didn't like, and somehow I managed to lose this. I remember waiting and waiting in this huge hall, being collected by Aunt Zdena, already in London after getting away the day before the Czech border closed. She took me by train to my new home, but I have absolutely no recollection of any time spent with her in her London home first.

My next memory is of standing in the corridor of the final train. I'm looking at the new scenery, nose to the dirty glass, mouthing phrases in English that I'd been taught. "Thank you, please, good morning," I practice saying to myself. After that, my chief memories are of arriving as a strange child, the center of attention, then bitter, chronic homesickness, and new people trying to distract me from eternal crying.

Prague

12th August 1939

My dear Mrs Campbell,

Now imagine, have you heard THAT I HAVE GOT MY PERMIT? The second one that was applied for some two weeks ago. Imagine the quickness! And how marvellous. I have immediately written to Miss H. (one of the Guiders in the Midlands) and asked about different particulars, before I start to do anything with it. The Permit is for the Midlands, I think there are some prescriptions that I must first go to the place from where the permit is applied for.

This I am not sure. Further, I am not sure how long I must stay in this place before I change for another. Then I am not sure how it will be with the married couple matter when this has occurred in the meantime. That is why I am not going to the Consul here and am waiting for news from Miss H and from Elsie.

I do not know if you can apply for Emil separately for domestic service. This would be very interesting to know. If he can get a Domestic Work Permit just as well as I, a single one, then there would be no bother and I could leave first and he could follow. I could come and do my duties with you, and then he would come and do his duties. I do not know if you would agree to this, that I would come at first separately.

When I start to do something with it here I can count about four weeks before I can leave. So that must be taken into consideration, so that you know with what you have to count. If you would like me to come quicker, then I should try another way. If Emil could not get a single Domestic Work Permit, then it would be more advisable for us to wait both together here for this Permit, because, there would then no more be any chance for Emil to get him over.

I wonder what Elsie will hear from Bloomsbury House. If matters would be so quick with the married couple Permit as they were with this one I got yesterday, then it would not much matter if we should wait. It is only a question when exactly your married couple will leave. If it were not otherwise possible I should then leave without Emil. But this must be well reflected.

At any rate, I am now waiting for news from you and Elsie before I do any further steps here. Because once I start here it can't be retained then (the flat) and I MUST leave. Also there is the question of the furniture etc. This is an affair on its own. Please could you be kind enough to tell me the measurements of the two rooms and if there can be put something in the kitchen. Where do the people wash? Oh, could you be perhaps so kind as to draw me the rooms that I have an idea of them. It is of course not the chief thing, but I am so interested, I always was of these things most interested when we had to change our flat. How is the wife (the Receptionist) dressed? Just in ordinary clothes, or do you want her to put on something special.

Now I must answer your letter. We are not at all afraid of the work, with this we must count everywhere, and we want to do all to make you satisfied. We mean it perfectly earnestly and with full conscience of what you want us to do. My husband was perfectly thrilled by the proposal. It really was the single thing we could wish, because it is the only way how we all three can be together. With £2 per week it is VERY WELL possible to manage for three persons here, and although I know that the conditions in England are different and the level of the prices is a little higher, I think if I shall be careful, that I can manage with this quite well. I have not well the idea, but I shall do my best to be economical. We have always lived, even here, in a very modest way, so it is not difficult for us to continue. We did not go out much, Emil rather likes to listen to his wireless and smoke his pipe. And there was also a time already in my life when I had to be very economical too. So I am not at all afraid of this.

How is my girlie? I am sorry that she wants all the time the violin. Also in this I recognise her. I shall write her tonight about it. She was always alone, and that is the fault.

How will it be done for the school year now? Elsie told in one of her letters that she has reserved a place in school for her already, and that she wants to go to London with two friends to fetch Milena. It seems now very probable that I soon will come to England; if there with you I could then take Milena to live with me. So I think it would be good at any rate now to leave Milena to start with school in the Midlands, as I am afraid all her Aunties there would be disappointed to have not had her at all there. But again, to start in one place with school and continue in the other, I do not know if this is good. But maybe it will not matter and if things would remain as they are, that means if I should not have any other Permit, I should most probably be obliged first to go to the Midlands. Later I could take Milena back to you with me. I must leave this to you and Elsie to do what you think best.

I wanted to send Milena a parcel with the rest of the things, but now I shall wait and take them with me. I am going now for a week with my husband. If I hear from you or Elsie that I have to leave with this Permit then I shall. If there would be again something you would like me to tell Milena, please do it. I was so glad you told me this time so I can help you a little bit with this.

Yours,
Anka

Parník,
Česká Třebová,
16th August 1939
My dear Mrs Campbell,

I have just got your letter of the 13th, forwarded to me from Prague. It seems to me that you have not got my letter which I wrote on the same day when I heard that your married couple post has become vacant. That was Friday week. By my answer I have told you that I should be only too happy to be able to get this post, and this letter crossed with your long letter where you told me all the details yourself, and which I have got on Wednesday last. I did not hurry to answer this letter of yours because I had the feeling that I could not write anything new than I have written already in my last letter.

I thought one or two days I'll leave the matter in case I should hear some further news as to the Permit. But on Friday I got from Miss H. my Permit. On Saturday I wrote to you, and I do hope that if you would not have got my former letter that you have understood from this letter of mine that we are perfectly happy to have got your offer and that we want to do our UTMOST to make you satisfied with us. We mean it earnestly with the WORK and you need not be afraid that we should not be able to do it. Please be so kind and do wait for us until we come! Please do not take another couple! I should not like to loose this marvellous chance which is offered to us by this proposal of yours—by a small misunderstanding caused maybe by a late reply.

But I really had the impression that you have got the answer already in the moment when I read your letter asking me for my, or our, decision. We have well reflected the matter and I feel perfectly sure that you will NOT regret when you take us. Elsie says that we can easily live with the £2 for all three of us, and that is such a great comfort to us, that even the child could be again with us and we ourselves could gain so much that she could live with us. This really is the most ideal solution, which we could wish. And if I was not sufficiently clear as to this in both my former letters and the one Post Card, then please excuse me. Maybe I felt overwhelmed by joy. The only thing now is the Permit of Emil, and also MY Permit.

My Permit is for a job in the Midlands and I do not know if it will be necessary to go first there, and how long I am forced to stay there before I may leave to come to you. And if then it would be too late to start the job with you!! That would be awful! Could your married couple wait until I should arrive? Second and very important matter—the second half of the new 'married couple'—Emil!! Can you get a second Work Permit (as for Butler or so) for him? Or is it necessary that you apply for BOTH of us together once more? Is it possible that another miracle happens and that another Permit goes so quickly through as mine which I have just got? If I know that Emil will get his Permit, it does not matter if it is later, then I shall leave as quickly as I can, without Emil, and he will follow when his Permit comes through. The single matter is, if YOU can have me alone in the beginning. I should be glad to have Emil soon there as he means a very great help to me. He is such a help to me in the household when I have no maid, you have no idea. And I'm sure that in the new conditions he would proof (I do not know how to spell it) as very useful. But I am NOT afraid to start with my work alone!!

Another thing I have asked in my first letter; IF I do not get my furniture through, and should arrive without it, IF THAT WOULD BE AN OBSTACLE? Pots and small things I can take at any rate, I think, furniture perhaps too, but it is not yet sure. I am waiting for your reply in this respect. I have started to work on this and to prepare. I am in the country with Emil, but I have not stopped 'work' to get the matter quickly through. As soon as I get the news that I have to leave with MY Permit and that there is hope to get a Permit for Emil then too, I shall return to Prague and shall start with full steam to realise all what I have been now working on.

It has been pouring ever since I have arrived here. But my humour is not affected by this.

Milena again writes a very cheerful letter describing how you have sent 'lists' to London because of me, and if we should be lucky, then the Gentleman in London would send me the Permit. But, she says 'all at once as a blow of thunder, Auntie came into the room with the news that I HAVE already got the Permit to be able to follow her.' Isn't it marvellous that Milena understands so much. I always thought she would be rather quick with languages, because she learnt SO quickly German, but still, when I think that nobody can explain to her in Czech what is said to her in English, it seems so strange that she gets the idea of what is spoken.

I do hope that you understand all and am anxiously waiting for further news. I am really curious as to Emil, because a lady here told me, that it IS possible to get a Domestic Work Permit for a man too, which I did not know. I thought that the only Permit that is given to a man is either as husband and wife for 'Married Couple's' job, or to a 'Skilled Worker' who is without competition in his line. For instance if he would get a post in a Hotel with his languages and they would not be able to get an Englishman with the knowledge of these languages, there COULD be a Permit obtained for him. I do not know if it is right, it would be necessary to have it confirmed at the respective Authorities in London. With many heartiest thanks and good wishes for your health. How are you feeling?

With much love,

Yours, Anka

Letters between mainland Europe and Britain had to travel by boat and rail and took at least three days, and why the Germans still permitted their free passage is a mystery. I don't remember if we had a telephone—they were still an uncommon luxury—and the cost of overseas calls would have been prohibitive even if such calls had been possible.

In the following letter, the last before war breaks out on September 3, there are an unprecedented number of underlinings of sentences and writings in the margins. My mother's anxiety and the urgency of the situation are palpable.

Parník,
Tuesday 22nd August 1939
Dear Mrs Campbell,

I have been so glad to have got your very nice letter of the 17th, by which you have told me that you want to wait for me and that you apply for the double Permit, etc etc. Also Milena sounds very happy in her last letter; she writes 'I like it here very much, it is here very nice, I am very well. 'And of the whole letter it is to be seen that she is in a very good humour. We both, Emil and I, have been so happy when the letter arrived. Thank you also for the snaps, and also very much for the plan and suggestions of what I have to take.

If only I could distinguish words like dresser, sideboard, cupboard, wardrobe, I should be glad. Elsie was always teasing me with those words. Once she made an explication and made drawings, to tell me the difference. I think I am not mistaken when I think that wardrobe is the piece of furniture the clothes are put in. But that the small table beside the bed you call 'cupboard'; you see I should never have thought! I thought into a cupboard, cups and saucers etc were put, i.e. I should have put it into the kitchen. Well the main thing is, that you suggest me to bring a sideboard. Please could you tell me what it is for and how it looks like in England. Is it not something similar as the dresser?

Do I well understand that the dresser you describe is permanently installed in the room, that means it does not belong to the couple. I have in my dining room such a thing; [here she draws a thirties-style matching pair of rectangular-shaped walnut cabinets, describing their contents as, behind the upper sliding glass doors, glasses and china and, behind the

Wien, Tuesday 22nd Aug.
1939

I have been so glad to have got your very nice
letter of the 17th, ~~and~~ by which [have]
[illegible] wait for me and that you
double P. etc etc. Also Milenka sounds very
happy ~~of~~ in her last letter; she writes ~~that~~ – „I like it
here very much, it is here very nice, I am very
well." And of the whole letter it is to be seen
that she is in a very good humour. We both,
Emil and I, have been so happy when the letter
arrived. Thank you also for the snaps, and also very
much for the plan and suggestions of what I have
to take. If only I should distinguish the words like
dresses, sideboard, cupboard, wardrobe, I should be
glad. Already D.C. was always ~~teas~~ teasing me with
these words. ~~It~~ once she made ~~me~~ an explication to
me and drawings to it, to tell me the difference. I think
I am not mistaken when I think that wardrobe is the piece
of furniture the clothes are put in. But that ~~is~~ the small
table beside the bed you call „cupboard", you see I should
have never thought! I thought ~~cups~~ into a cupboard
cups and saucepans etc were put, i.e. ~~that~~ I should have
put it into the kitchen. Well the main thing is, that
you suggest ~~to~~ me to bring a side board. Please could
you tell me what it is for and how it looks like in
England. Is it not something similar as the dresser?
Do I well understand that the dresser you describe
is permenantly installed in the room, that means
it does not belong to the couple. I have in my
dining room such a thing: [glass] otherwise all the doors of wood, I put china and glas and table cloths etc into it
This I intend to bring and then
if possible the piano, wireless, gram. and sewing machine, 2 armchairs
table and small chairs. I do hope that on the wall you
suggested for the „sideboard" I can put ~~my~~ the described (above)
piece of furniture and the piano. The above thing is 6 feet 4 long
and the piano I think 4 feet and 5'6", may be only 4 feet. I am in
Pasnik and do not know it by heart exactly.

lower walnut-veneer doors, tablecloths, etc.]. And what is a dresser for? Where do you put food, flour, stores of marmalades etc? I have a small laundry room for it.

This I intend to bring, and if possible the piano, wireless, gramophone, and sewing machine. Two armchairs, table and small chairs. I do hope that on the wall you suggested for the 'sideboard' I can put the piece of furniture described above and the piano. The above thing (actually two cabinets standing together) is six feet four long, and the piano I think four feet. I am in Parník and do not know it by heart exactly. Have I well understood that in case I should not bring a bed for Milena, you would lend yours? Thank you very much indeed, but in case I should be able to send other furniture then I should bring a bed or couch for her too.

In case there would arise some difficulties in sending off the furniture, I should just try to send at least the most important pieces, not in a lift van, as it is done, but separately packed. This will show the next week.

I am waiting here till Sunday and on Monday I am leaving for Prague and shall start with the work combined with the removal and departure. Till this time I do hope to get news either from my sister or Elsie and also further news from you which I shall then judge if I have to come on my own on a single Permit, or wait for a double Permit.

Please could you be kind enough to send me with your next letter also an official letter with 'Dear Mrs Rothová', where you would tell me that it is essential for the future work with you that I bring my sewing machine and that with this presumption you have accepted me. This I need, as we can bring any machines only if we need them for our future work.

She added:

Mid day pause. Emil just brought your letter of the 20th and the letter from the country, of the 11th! This letter was altogether 11 days going, I have had the impression all the time that ONE letter, either mine or yours got lost, and now here is the answer to that where I repeated what my sister wrote me. I am so happy that you are not afraid to use my work. But as I said before, I shall do what I can and really hope quite sincerely that I shall get accustomed to the work and that my goodwill to do it well, will succeed. Still something; what is a HOT cupboard? And 'Safe' for meat is something I presume, where meat can be put not to become bad. A cold place it is, isn't it? You will laugh at me but I can't help it, I don't know the words, I have no Dictionary here and maybe I should not find these words in there.

In case I CAN bring my furniture and in case one or the other piece would not go into my two rooms, is there a place in the house (loft or something) where I could have it stored? If I can take the furniture it would be better to take as much as such a liftvan takes, it is with the same expense, and here what we leave is lost, and there on the worst we can sell it. But don't be afraid that I should bring very much more, just one or two pieces I think, as more will not go in the five metres liftvan. I must measure still everything. How long is the wall in the kitchen where you suggest the table? From door to draining wood? If possible I should take a SMALL table and narrow wardrobe for ordinary clothes etc.

I am looking forward to seeing you, and once I'll get over the sad part of the matter—leaving my people and my country—I shall feel quite happy, I think. Emil has given me different questions as to your garden, etc which I could not answer to. He said that so as I am interested in the rooms, wardrobe, sideboards, etc, so he is of what is connected with HIS work.

Milena wrote in her last letter six times underlined 'Dear Mummy and Daddy. It is here AWFULLY NICE'. I wonder how she will like it in the Midlands? Have you had a nice talk with Elsie? Zdena wrote that she, Elsie, has lost her dog in London. The dog I think I remember when I was last time in England. Like your Boytsam!

When I get to Prague I shall make a legalised English translation of Milena's Birth Certificate and shall send it to you.

Zdena has written today that she as well as Elsie have asked at Bloomsbury House and they were told that I have to leave with MY Permit and you (the employer) can then ask or apply for Emil. So I am immediately proceeding with my part of the matter and I do hope that nothing will arise to prolong my departure. And maybe that before I leave the Double Permit will arive and that we shall leave together. I intend to take a part of Emil's things, suits etc, with the other things.

Thank you very much for your offer that Milena could have meals with you, if I wish. We shall see this when once I am there, at any rate I do not intend to make you any special extra expenses if it should not be necessary. I am so grateful for all your winks [*sic*]. It will be a great help for me in the beginning because even the way as for instance meat is shopped and sold here is another way than in your country. Some food is here less expensive, another less in England. This all must show the experience.

I am glad that Mrs Mathewson has written you nicely and that she is not angry that she had to wait for such a long time in vain. But she has understood I am sure.

I think that I shall be able to leave something ROUND ABOUT THE 20th SEPTEMBER. I don't think it will be quicker, but I do hope will not take longer. At any rate there can't be a great difference. Just a question of a few days, SOONER or LATER. So I do hope that till that time you will be able to wait for me with daily help. The only question still is, IF I am allowed to go straight to you to work with you, when I have got a Permit to work in the Midlands. I know I am allowed to change the post, but it is a question if I am allowed to do it straight away. I hope Elsie will tell me.

With much love,

Yours, Anka

Still something, (have opened the envelope once more because of this)—any work even that which you did not mention and will want me to do for you I am gladly willing to do.

Into which class will you put Milena? I should not like her to loose [*sic*] a year, and so should be glad if you would put her with children of the SAME age, just like if she would know English well. In the first time she'll not know much, but she'll get accustomed and you'll see that it will do. She has learnt at school very well, she counts nicely for her age, (for our country, I do not know how much your children must already know at this age, every country has another plan in the schools.) So I do hope that she will do in the English school also well. Please put her to a free school (without paying) so that she can continue there when I come. I think that the schools I have seen in the Midlands were all free schools and they were very well equipped and the children there were nice.

Must stop, shall write still to Elsie and my daughter.

Once more,

Much love from Anka

It is interesting to conjecture how a child perceives happiness. I have noticed that children and young people can seem immensely cheerful on the surface, and indeed when I look at letters written by me at that time and later, they are full of jokes.

But the day I was left in my new home, I embarked on a week of non-stop crying for my parents, day and night. Doris complained that it was very inconvenient, because she couldn't go out and leave me like that with the maid. I remember playing a primitive game of mud pies in the garden; I can actually still see myself, sqatting down at the edge of a flower bed, digging up some sloppy wet earth with a trowel and trying to form pies with it. There is a fleeting memory of thinking myself into a time before I was born, feeling as if I could remember it—an odd sensation—and then writing in a diary that I had managed to last a whole day without crying. About fifty years later, Doris told me that I had written to my mother saying that I was mad with longing for her. From then on, I was crippled with homesickness at every move. I could not stay away from my new home for even a week without getting ill with it.

I think my newfound family tried to distract me with books: both Doris and her husband Arthur tried to read to me, in English. I didn't mind that. I was introduced right away to Beatrix Potter, which I loved. I still have those 1926 editions that had belonged to the Campbells. My favorite was *The Tailor of Gloucester,* for the beauty of the fabric and embroidery and the pathos of the story. Already I could identify with tragedy! Years later, Jane and I went up to the attic and rescued these books, which were about to be disposed of, and she gave them to me. Of course I have them still, and I read them to my own children and now my grandchildren.

I remember early on in this new home being given some columns of figures to add up—I was a whiz at these. The Campbells had never looked after a child without a nanny, and now, at a time when their own children were just finishing at boarding school, they were faced, instead of with a new working couple, with a foreign six-and-a-half-year-old. I was a problem and a nuisance.

During this first month I was also sent away to spend time with my mother's other friends. Elsie was the schoolteacher who had offered to look after my education; she lived with her mother and kept a close watch on me. I can remember the close scrutiny in this home, even more than in Doris's. In Elsie's, I was a much-welcomed child for a lonely woman. I also had to sleep sharing her bed, but nothing worse than that happened as far as I can remember.

However, unbeknownst to me, the English women embarked on a correspondence, which I still have as well, deploring my behavior—I was disloyal to my mother and country, I made facetious remarks—and arguing the merits of various forms of upbringing. I developed a facial twitch, blinking my eyes. This caused more disagreement and a spate of conflicting diagnoses, none of which included recent emotional trauma, although Elsie did suggest that I might be "emotionally unstable," which Doris hotly refuted. The level of my intelligence was disputed, too. Elsie saw me as clever and talented, ready for her superior education; to Doris, I was certainly no better than her own children. I did or did not need glasses. The twitch should be cured by being ignored. Finally I was given a penny if I didn't twitch all day. This ignorance and insensitivity was normal for the time, and unsurprisingly the plan to share me among the friends soon broke down.

My own positive attitude to my new life must have been fueled in part by my belief that I would soon see my parents again, and strengthened by the residual ebullience I'd brought from home. I certainly cannot remember any actual happiness, more a sort of automatic going through the motions of living, but possibly enjoying some of the new experiences. I could always laugh; you don't have to be happy to do that. There was, however, an overwhelming sensation of strangeness. I certainly was a strange phenomenon in my new home and environment, an oddity, and, worse still, remained one.

I did not actually lack attention; I often thought, then and now, that I had too much. I was much too visible. That way I could get into trouble; it also added to my feeling of being different. I liked it best when the Campbell children came home for the holidays and I could peacefully merge into the background, and trouble could be spread more thinly.

All the furniture my mother describes survived the war, was kept safely in Prague by friends, and was sent to me by Zdena and my uncle, who returned to live in Prague very soon after the war ended. It has been in my own use ever since. Only this week, while writing this book, it occurred to me to ask my aunt for the first time, "Who looked after it all those years?"

She told me an interesting story. My mother had asked a non-Jewish Czech Girl Guide if she would look after it, and this Guide passed it on to her married brother. He did indeed house it throughout the war and the occupation of Prague by the Germans. After returning to live in Prague, my aunt felt she should reclaim the furniture for me and visited this brother and his wife. The wife was perturbed and felt she couldn't part with it. "The neighbors might tell the authorities that we have been harboring the furniture of Jews." So they had taken a serious risk in doing this and could have been reported by anti-Semitic neighbors and sent to a concentration camp for doing so. Now she had forgotten that the Nazis were no longer in power. Also maybe she needed the furniture, and had grown used to it. Many people who looked after Jews' belongings refused to part with them afterwards. Some even denied knowledge of having any.

My aunt visited the brother's sister and told her the story, and she prevailed with her sister-in-law. My uncle then did the paperwork, and one day, in a wooden liftvan, my furniture arrived. All the glass and china were packed inside, quite intact. All of it has survived its journeys across Europe, around England, to wherever I moved. Thus my mother's preoccupation with these belongings was not so futile. They did form a very real thread of continuity between us. And they did reach England as she intended.

When I first read all her anxious queries about the furniture, my mind boggled. Here is a family desperately seeking to flee for survival, but still the dimensions of her furniture preoccupy her to the extent of detailing it in letters to her rescuer. And I know that Doris regarded this as entirely normal and answered all the questions as a matter of course. She thought of her own belongings in the same way. The furnishings were in fact status symbols in a very deep and necessary way. In that time of extreme peril, when even if my mother survived, she would have become a maid and lost all evidence of her former home and culture, the significance of these symbols became even more important. Similarly, their survival has been of greater importance to me than would otherwise have been normal in my own life.

I use this furniture every day and feel a satisfying sense of connection with her. The desk in particular is in front of me now, filled with the files and papers of everyday life. The lower section, behind the famous walnut-veneer doors, is filled with sewing equipment. The drop-down shelf, on which people used to write their letters, is stained with old ink. It could be the ink of the people who looked after the furniture during the war, as I never write at a desk, only at a table. Or it might be my mother's, since some of these letters were handwritten. That gives me a comforting feeling. At the top, behind the sliding glass doors, are the spare paper and disks that I need for this book. So the desk has been used for the whole of my life, and this matters when all else has been broken. Funnily enough, despite their sentimental value, I've always considered the cabinets to be ugly. But now that thirties furniture is all the thing, they seem to me quite elegant!

And, on further reflection, I realize that such objects were seen as somehow more "permanent" in those days. You got your dowry when you married, set yourself up for life, and the furniture, linen, glass formed part of the persona of yourself and the home, and was passed on to your children. There was a sort of "rightness" to it all that feels very Germanic (and was even passed on to the British through Germanic Victorianism). It formed a sort of family solidity, a totem. In fact, the attachment to furniture was so prevalent that some Jews lost their lives because they couldn't bring themselves to leave until the passage of their furniture was assured.

Whenever I see a Germanic person (whether German, Austrian, or Swiss), they all seem to have this aura of certainty. I see them perform a simple task, whether carving meat, serving pastries in a shop, or performing precise domestic tasks, and what comes to mind is that certainty of "rightness," of one's actions never being called into question, certainly not subject to any struggles of conscience, and I wonder upon how many centuries such convictions have been built. The Jews having had all certainty removed, and even our very being (by the Germans themselves), this clinging to the symbols of status is the most natural response in the world. I know that when I see anyone possessed of such certainty today, I still feel a pang of envy.

Germany invaded Poland on September 1, and on September 3 Britain and France declared war on Germany. All legal movement of Jews in Europe was at once stopped, and my parents were therefore trapped, fearing that they would never see me again.

As always, my mother understates the situation and writes as if there might soon be a good outcome, but it is nevertheless clear that she knows better.

Interestingly, she now feels able to state in her next letter, for the first time, that she intends to use Doris's first name.

Prague,
9th September 1939
My dear Doris,

I have not had any news of you since about ten days. I do hope that all goes on normally, and that you are much better already after your surgery. I have been thinking of you very much in the last days. Probably you are at home, or in the nursing home. Milena is also there isn't she.

I feel awfully sorry that I could not leave in time. It means that I shall live in great sorrows and unquietness, when she is there and I am here. Well nothing can be done. I know perfectly well that she is in the best hands she can be at all, but also for you, I am afraid, it will mean a great sorrow. Let us hope that it will not last a too long time, and that then we shall all meet happily. Have you taken a new married couple? Because with my departure we cannot count, of course. We all must take things as they are. I shall remove the furniture to my mother in law's, she has made me room there, and then in October I shall go and join my husband.

Please if possible do write me soon.

I am sending school books for Milena, so that she can learn of them. I know that it will be very difficult for her, to do it without me, but perhaps she could just read it either from the school book or a fairy tale and copy a bit of it. She makes lovely mistakes in orthography, which can be 'cured' maybe by this method. I have told her to do this if possible every second day. Please do as you think best and if it is not possible, leave it.

With kindest regards and best wishes. I do hope you are recovering already after the operation.

Yours as ever, Anka

I shall now always use your Christian name, instead of your surname. I do hope you'll excuse and understand.

In saying that she is afraid "it will mean a great sorrow" for Doris, she refers to the fact that Doris had two sons of military age.

Presumably my father was either in the country or at his mother's house, outside Prague, where it might have been easier to find work and he would have had free accommodations. Or maybe, because Jewish men were already in danger of being picked up and sent away by the Nazis, it was safer in the country altogether.

The outbreak of war was announced on the British radio news at 11 A.M. in an atmosphere of some drama. Usually I went with the family to church at that hour, but this time we remained at home, because, I believe, bombs were expected right away. We all knew that this was the beginning of very big trouble, and I realized at once that it would mean my parents would not be able to join me. Having always known that I had been sent away to save my life from a bad man called Hitler who didn't like Jews, I knew that my parents' lives were also in danger and that it was possible we would not meet again.

One of the problems, therefore, was which life I was to adapt to—a return to Prague and everything Czech, or to become English? I was consciously aware of this conflict very soon; I felt it acutely. I think it brought me nearer to feeling mentally ill than had any other problem. The utter confusion and threat.

The English world may have been hostile to me personally as a foreigner and a Jew, but it was less threatening to my feelings than the hothouse terror of the Czech relations. And because each culture was suspicious of the other, and mistrusted my identification with it, I literally didn't know where to turn. And there was guilt, in terms of disloyalty, whichever way I turned. I think that I was already so disoriented that my homesickness became a sort of chronic grief, and indeed, even now, when moved without my own volition from any place which I feel is home, I can sustain homesickness to a profound and longstanding degree. And when I am in a milieu with which I can't mentally identify, I feel threatened and chronically uneasy—not physically, but mentally—and can't easily live with the difference.

And, in any case, we were not to know for six years what the outcome would be, so we all lived in a state of uncertainty and, in a way, suspended animation.

For Doris there was the anxiety of coping with impending war and the possible mobilization of her sons, who had just left school, plus the utter nuisance of being saddled with a young child, perhaps permanently, in place of the domestic help she had been anticipating. There was no question of my studying the Czech books my mother was so anxious I should use to retain my mother tongue. Understandably, that was not a priority.

Prague,
22nd November 1939
My dear Doris,

As you see I am still in Prague. Míla will have her wedding on Sunday next so I shall help here. Then next Tuesday or Wednesday I hope to return to Emil, just for four weeks, because, as I told you last time, he has got notice from his work and we shall remove back to Prague again. I have baked different little cakes for the wedding and shall do the same today and tomorrow. Today we went to buy a hat for Míla. She has a lovely blue coat and we shall buy a hat of the same colour.

The last letter we have got from Mr Shapira goes through the post very quickly comparatively. From C.K. (Switzerland?) the letters get greater delay. From Stockholm post goes very irregularly and in fact yours did not arrive at all this way. Last time I wrote to C.K. it took full nine days. That is a lot.

Nevertheless I am much quieter since I got your last news and even if I should not get letters regularly I hope to keep a bit calm. I am so glad all is in order with you and Milena.

Do you need sometimes the Dictionary? Did you use it much in the beginning? If it were possible just to see you all for half an hour like in the moving picture. It would be such fun for me to hear Milena talking. The books are 'en route' I have been told, so that soon Milena will have some Czech books to read.

Thank you ever so much for all the trouble I am causing you. All words are too small to express all I feel. Milena did not much like the porridge here, but I do hope she will get accustomed to it. I too, when I ate it for the first time at a Guide camp in Geneva, I did not like it at all, and later I always had two helpings and had it at home done separately for me.

My sister has the dressmaker in the house just today so there is a lot of fuss in the house. I shall have quite a lot to do for the wedding. Please could you tell Milena to write on her letters always both Dear Mummy and Daddy because Emil is sad when she writes only to me.

I must close now.

With all my love,

yours, Anka

P.S. Could you please tell Milena to read aloud sometimes from the books.

There is also a note scribbled at the bottom in pencil from the intermediary who passed on this letter:

Madam,

With the second mail I got your letter too, which I am passing at once to Mrs Rothová.

Kindest regards,

J Shapira

One way in which the Germans were gradually making it impossible for the Jews to survive was to stop them from practicing their businesses and professions. She mentions the loss of both their jobs; I don't know what they were living on, or whether they were still in the block of flats she managed where they had lived rent-free.

There seem to have been several intermediaries through whom mail was sent: one in Switzerland, one in Yugoslavia, one in Sweden. It was still legal to send letters to countries that were then neutral. My family must have had their own personal or business contacts, for all their messages were in the form of normal letters. Whereas the Red Cross, which also facilitated the passage of letters to other countries, provided small postcards on which only a limited message could be written.

The tiny handwritten notes from the intermediaries on some of the letters show them to have been fully involved and rather sweetly helpful. This little postcard (dated October 11, 1939) I've recently noticed—I've had these things for so long, and taken them so much for granted as the background wallpaper of my life—that, as with the letter from Ela's father, I'm slow to see their significance:

Dear Madam,

I am writing in the name of Mrs Rothová, mother of little Milena. She asks you to be so kind and write her on my address. I shall forward your kind letter. She has no news of her little daughter and is very anxious to know, how Milena is, wether [*sic*] she is in good health and wether you are satisfied with her. She sends you kindest regards and thanks you so much for your kindness.

Yours truly
Dr C. Kalan
Celve
Miklošičevá
Ulica 6
Yougoslavia

The following letter is the first recorded letter that I have (written in English by my mother) which my parents wrote directly to me. I'm sure there must have been earlier ones, as I had been in England for more than a year by the time this was written, but since her letters were being sent via these intermediaries in Switzerland, Yugoslavia, or

Sweden, it is quite likely that some didn't get through, or it's possible that Doris left some letters addressed to me in my care and that I, as a young child, lost them. Doris tended to be meticulous about keeping letters.

Sunday 18th August 1940

My dear Mileno,

It is now such a very long time since I heard from you the last time. About two months. You should write by airmail, so that we can get it quicker. What are you doing all the time and how are you? This week is your last week of holidays, isn't it? I would very much like to know how you are getting on, how you have enjoyed your holidays and whether you are looking forward to go to school again.

Now you are going to be in the fourth standard, since you once told us you were in the third, or am I wrong? Please write a nice, and very long letter, either in Czech or in English, as ever you want. The best would be to write a bit in Czech and the whole rest in English and that way you can make the letter longer in English. Do you want me to write in English too?[1] But maybe that my English is not so nice as yours and that you will find in my English mistakes. That is all possible. Because I have not spoken English for a very long time already, so I have forgotten a lot. I have been reading now the Forsyte Saga, an English book. It has got 6 volumes. I am reading just now the 5th volume. So I shall soon have it finished.

We are all all right. I cook for all and now I have been making all sorts of jams, so I have been very busy. If I had you here it would be a great help for me. Grandma had some tomatoes in her garden, but not as many as we had hoped.

Auntie Lisa had her holidays, but she did not go anywhere. Grandma was afraid she would be too lonely, so Auntie Lisa stayed at home. We did not go to the country either, none of us. It was not a pity, since it had been rather cold all the time. Yesterday Daddy and I was on the farm where Daddy used to go in the Spring. The dog Osina, I think you have written about her before, has had four young puppies. They were yester-

Můžeš poslouchat, jak Judith hraje ale ~~xxxx~~ nesmíš už to chtít. Aneb jinou věc, kterou se Ti nechce dát, nesmíš podruhé chtít. To také je neposlušnost, když se vždy znovu chce to samé.

Když Ti dají něco k jídlu, co neznáš, nebo co se Ti nezdá být dobré, tak neříkej nikdy , Milenko,"This is not good."
Víš co to znamená? To znamená, že se to kazí, že snad už je to plesnivé, nebo nahnilé, zkrátka špatné. Tak si to pamatuj, ~~když~~ o jídle se neříká " This is not good". Když se Ti to jídlo ~~ix~~ nelíbí anebo když Ti nechutná, řekni :"Auntie, I do not like it!" To znamená: Já to nemám ráda, nebo mně to nechutná. Tak si to pamatuj , mrňavko.

Jinak je zde vše v pořádku. Opět přiložím jeden lístek a můžeš napsat opět babičce , že je v Třebové lepší než v Praze. To se Ti povedlo. Taky pro tetu Lisu něco připiš.

Jsem ráda, že se Ti dobře daří a že jsi u tak hodné tetičky a strýčka. Jen buď stále hodná, aby Tě měli stále rádi.

Zítra ráno jedu za tatínkem do Třebové a zůstanu tam asi týden. Napíšu Ti odtamtud delší dopis. Jenže tam nemám stroj, tak Ti to dá práci, než to přečteš. Ještě chce napsat teta Lisa něco, tak musím přestat.

Posílám Ti padesát tisíc pus jako hrom.

Jak se těšíš do školy? Jsem na Tebe zvědavá, jak Ti to půjde. Ale doufám, že dobře a že se Ti tam určitě bude líbit.

Tvoje maminka

Nazdar Mrňousku. Co děláš? Přijela jsem minulý týden ze Staměřic. Ten chlapeček, co tam mají, měl z těch hraček, co jsi mu poslala, velkou radost. - Už jsem Ti uháčkovala k jedné košilce moc hezkou kraječku. Babička pořád myslí, že jsi v Třebové a z tvého posledního lístku měla velkou radost. Je ráda, že se Ti dobře daří.
Pořád na Tebe vzpomínáme a jsme rádi, že nám tetička píše, že jsi hodná holčička. Zase nám něco napiš .

Mockrát tě pozdravuje Tvoje teta LISA

jedu k tatínkovi a on už na mne čeká a mává

day only one day old. The mother lapped and nursed them all the time, so that they were warm. They were very sweet.

The decorator, who had our doggy Sam, told me the other day that he would have another dog. Did you get my letter where I told you that Sam didn't live any more? He has been killed by a car. So I think the decorator will have one of these puppies.

They have not got many chickens on the farm, they died suffering from indigestion. Daddy was very sad when he heard the news. He was looking forward to see the chickens how they have grown since he last saw them.

The other day we were busy with Daddy a whole afternoon sticking some of the snaps of you into an album. Some more are still missing, and I will find them and complete the album. It will be a nice souvenir for you one day when you are grown up.[2]

Can you still wear your frocks you had last year? They all could be made bigger, so I hope you can. I use to look at little girls who are as old as you are, and I compare them with you to be able to imagine how big you are now. Would you know me and Daddy and Auntie Lisa and Grandma and Auntie Míla and Uncle Arnošt, if you saw us? I had a dream the other day: You came home for holidays and I said to you; 'Well, since you look very well and you like it there so much, you can go to Auntie Doris for another school year'. You can think how you and I and Daddy was full of joy to see each other again.

I must finish now. There is a gentleman here to see us and they all play 'flees.' I do not know whether you know this game. How are Jane, Harry and James? And is the Uncle all right? I am going to write a separate letter to Auntie. Please remember me to all of them.

An enormous kiss from your MAMMY

You asked in a letter when is my birthday. Mine is the 24th November, and Daddy's is correctly on the 10th November. We both have our birthday in the same month.

1. Doris made a list of questions to ask my mother, one of which was did I want her to write to me in English. Doris effectively knew no Czech, and would have had to get Czech letters translated for me. I was fluent in English by then and don't remember how much Czech I had retained. In any case, it was a six-and-a-half-year-old's Czech.

2. The photo album they made for me did not survive.

Now a letter from my father, which is literally the only direct memento that I have of him, apart from photos:

Dear Mileno,

Last week I went with some little girls to the country, so I thought of you, how your holidays turned out this year. Here the children have their holidays since the middle of June, but these little girls went for August. On the beginning of September they will go home again, because in the beginning of September they go to school again. Three of them I brought home again, because they were ill.

Kindest regards from your Daddy

The address my mother gave Doris is what she called "my husband's address, Mr Emil Roth, exportní odd. fy.H. Pollacka synové. Parník, Třebová, Bohemia." This, I believe, must have been where some of her cousins had a textile factory, and perhaps my parents, or at least my father, found work and shelter there.

The following letter, written directly to me by my mother, is the last I received from her. It is written in Czech and was translated by an English friend many years later, long after I could understand it. In fact, I am surprised that I could understand it in November 1940, more than a year after leaving Prague. Yet if I was still writing to Grannie (my paternal grandmother) in Czech, I could not have forgotten the language as fast as I had thought.

November 18th 1940

Dear Mileno,

Many thanks for your very long letter. I gave away everything as you directed; 2 to grandfather, 2 to father, and one to grandmother. They were all very glad to get them from you.

Next time write on one side of the page only, as otherwise it creates problems when I have to cut it up (to give everyone your messages.)

Grandfather was delighted that you sent him so many kisses. Everyone sends you their greetings, even Miss Seamstress. She has made another pair of pyjamas for you. So I shall not send your things, because I shall probably visit you soon and bring them with me.

How do you like it there? How do you like English cooking? Now, I am not pleased that you don't like Jane. I wouldn't have thought it of you to be like that. One ought to like everybody and if you find it difficult, you must try not to show it. You are there as if you were at home, but you are a guest of your aunt and uncle and you must behave accordingly, and you should be nice to their sons and daughter. And when Jane doesn't want to lend you her violin, it's because she can't, not that she doesn't want to. This is a very expensive violin. She inherited it from her grandfather and it's very valuable. It isn't something for little children to play on. Jane is a big girl, and very talented musically, so she is allowed to play the violin, but one musn't play false notes on the violin or it scratches. The violin is then ruined and it would lose its beautiful sound. For learning and practicing one can buy a very cheap violin, but you are too small even for those. So write to me nicely whether you're good and that you no longer want the violin from Jane. You can't have everything you see when Auntie or Jane says 'No, I can't give you this.' You can listen to Jane playing but you mustn't want it, or any other thing which she doesn't want to give you. You mustn't want it. It is also disobedient when one keeps asking for the same thing.

When they give you something to eat that you don't know and don't fancy, don't ever say, Milena, 'This is not good.' Do you know what that means? It means that it has gone off, or is mouldy, altogether bad. So remember not to say 'this is not good' about food. If you dont like the food or the taste of it, say, 'Auntie, I do not like it', which means, 'I don't like it' or ' it's not to my taste.' So remember, little one.

Otherwise, everything is all right. Again I am enclosing a card and you can write again to Grandmother that it is nicer in Třebová than in Prague. So, you've succeeded.

Do add something to Auntie Lisa.

I'm glad you're keeping well and that you're with such a nice Auntie and Uncle. Be good, so they continue to like you.

Tomorrow morning I shall take the train to see Father in Třebová and I shall stay there probably for a week. I shall write you a longer letter from there. However, I don't have a typewriter there, so you will have to work to read it. Auntie Lisa would like to write something too, so I must stop. I'm sending you 50,000 kisses like lightning. Are you looking forward to school? I shall be interested to hear how you're doing, but I'm hoping you'll do well and really like it.

'troje maminka'- (from your little Mammy)

The comment about her coming to visit me soon is a total mystery to me. The dating may be wrong, as it was added in my own writing after its translation many years later, and I cannot find a date in her letter. It may have been written a year earlier. Some illegal escapes were still being made at that time, and she may have been plotting a last-ditch attempt. Since she had not brought me up on false hopes, she must have had some plan in mind, yet would it have been safe to write it in a letter?

In censuring my behavior while a guest in someone else's house, my mother seemed not merely anxious but almost frantic in case I should so alienate my hosts that they would either reject or dislike me. She had good reason, for she may have realized by now that she had not sent me to a tolerant house. My faults were swiftly made clear to me, and conditional acceptance was something that most child refugees experienced in contrast with their own homes that they'd left.

I was to write to my grandmother maintaining the deception that I remained in Czechoslovakia, in Tabor, where some of the family lived outside Prague. The idea of my having been sent abroad alone would have created havoc in Grannie's mind and maybe in the family. I was her only grandchild. This deception, encouraged by a mother who had taught me strictly not to lie, shows the desperation of those days.

My mother added a note to Doris:

Oh, I have forgotten to tell you, Milena wrote me in her letter, that she was NO more crying, and that she has much laughed when she read my letter. Her letter was very nice. She added a note for Babička, where she said that in Třebová the place my husband is, it was much nicer than in Prague. Babička was sad that Milena went to Třebová. Imagine, that the child has not forgotten this; and instead of 'In England it is nicer than in Prague', she wrote that. I must stop. It is again very late. So late that I dare not tell you the hour. But I shall leave tomorrow morning and who knows if I should be able to write immediately tomorrow, so I do it still today, not to lose much time.

My very best love,
yours, Anka

Auntie Lisa, my father's sister, adds a note to me:

Hallo little one,

How are you? I arrived here last week from Stameric. That little boy they have there had great pleasure from the toys you sent him. I've already knitted a collar for one of your shirts.[1] Grandma still thinks you're in Třebová, and she was very pleased with your last card and is pleased you're well. We're constantly thinking of you, and we're glad Auntie writes that you're a nice girl. Please write again.

Many greetings from your Auntie Lisa

1. Lisa did beautiful crochet work, which embellished even my underwear.

The following letter, the final one preserved, may or may not have been the last one sent or received. It is addressed to all my mother's friends and family in England and shows that the entire family had sought refuge with Grannie at Hloubětín, outside Prague.

I had already been in England for three years, and the war and the repression of Jews were fierce. It is remarkable that she managed to get any letters out to us at all. Up to the present, I have managed to piece together some details of their daily lives after my departure, from what people wrote or told me after the war, but gaps remain.

It is written via her intermediary in Switzerland, and she gives the address. This may account for her debate as to whether to write the letter in French.

Boulevard Dubois,
15 Rue Charles Girou,
Genève
July 21st, 1942
My dear, dear friends,

This letter is meant for all of you, as I am very busy and cannot write to each one a separate letter. Only Milena will get a part of the letter to her, as she has written us such a very long and nicely written letter, so she deserves her special letter.

Not so much Zdena, who did not write herself for months. If it were not that Doris tells us each time she writes, that you two are well, we should not even know if you are still alive. 'Take yourself together' (an idiom of my native tongue translated into English, I don't know whether used in English too.) and take off your laziness and put a few lines on paper for us when Doris and Milena write. You may write in English or in French, we both understand.

I should have written French today, as I intended to, but it does not 'flow out' of my pen so fluently as English so perhaps nobody of you will mind, will you! It is just three weeks ago since I posted my last letter to you, written in my native tongue. Since that day I have all the time in my mind to post another letter to you, written in French or English, because I know you understand this better but I could not. I have been much helping. All the family almost, is in the country, the school holidays having begun, and it has been a lot of work packing them up etc.

Arnošt's mother, Uncle Joseph, (my mother's brother) with Aunt Mary and the oldest aunt of our family, the sister of my grandmother 87 years old, you remember her still, Zdena, she used to live in Tabor, in the same house where our dear father went to school. She was living since March here in our town in an asylum for old people. Now they all live in the country, with Lisa and Milena's granny. Also our subtenants, all four of them are spending their time in the country.

You may imagine what fuss it was in the flat when such old people prepare themselves for a journey. But we have no time for holidays, so you may write us here, as always. Emil is very busy and Míla too; Arnošt[1] is taking care of the baby and their household, and I do all for us too. As

I do even all the washing, you may imagine that I am all the time busy. Besides that I am doing the same work as last summer. Three times a week the whole day, so I have not a spare moment left for myself.

Baby (Míla's boy, Pavel) is a fine jolly boy. It is a pleasure to look at him. But he ought to be fatter. Milena was, when so old, much fatter. But he eats well, Míla says he will be like his father, who eats a lot and still is rather thin. But otherwise he is strong, he keeps walking round his little bed all day long, never tired. He also wants to 'speak' something.

How is Dr Campbell? Is he all right again? I have been sorry to hear he has been so ill. How jolly it must have been when Harry arrived home after such a long time!

Now think I must stop, as I want to have this letter posted still today.

My very best regards to ALL my old good friends, and to you all much much love,

Anka

P.S. Ralph[2] is well. Adá's Aunt Zd. with family are all sending their love. Next time they too will write a few words.

1. Arnošt was my aunt Míla's husband, and my great favorite.

2. Ralph was the little boy I heard later they "adopted."

Although these letters traveled through Switzerland, the Swiss attitude toward Jews was unfriendly, despite Switzerland's claims to be a neutral nation. As early as September 1938, the Swiss authorities actually asked the German government to mark all Jewish passports with a large red *J* to prevent Jews from smuggling themselves into Switzerland.

Beyond the bare remarks in this letter, I know nothing of my parents' lives at this time or what her or Emil's work outside the home was, but now we have the image of all these frightened people, whose terror had communicated itself to me three years earlier, having had to flee their homes, and seek refuge in the country, and try, all the generations together, to live for a little longer.

Hindsight aside, there does seem to be an air of despairing farewell to this letter, as if my mother knew that the end, deportation, must be near. Whether any other letters were sent, I don't know, but this is the last I have.

4
Wartime in England

So all the while these sparse letters were coming, we were living through the war in England without any idea of conditions in Europe. Or should I say, I had no idea. But since the war tended to be discussed openly, I'm sure the adults around me knew only about the progress of the war in terms of the combat reported on radio and in newspapers. We lived from one BBC news bulletin to the next, in anxious anticipation. How many enemy aircraft had been shot down, how bad the effects of the previous day's bombing had been, what shortages of food or goods we should expect next. And of course a lot went unreported, especially anything that the enemy could use for its own benefit or that might lower the morale of the British people.

Despite what was known about Hitler's intentions toward the Jews, only Britain had allowed these 10,000 children to enter via the Kindertransport. The other countries closed the hatches when a large influx of refugees threatened, although they (in particular America) had allowed immigration of people with adequate financial means in the early and mid-thirties, in some cases as late as 1938. Without the pressure put on the British Parliament by Jewish and other leaders in 1938, we would not be here.

January 1942 was the last time my mother managed to get a letter through to us, and in July the Wannsee Conference was held, and the German Reinhard Heydrich had revealed an official plan to murder all the Jews on the European continent. I would think it very likely that my parents knew this when she wrote this last letter to us in July, and that would account for its tone of weary and tragic farewell.

Milena Roth, August 1939.

When I check my books again, I see that a chapter title in *Outlines of English History* for the year 1943 is "The Turn of the Tide." There was, on the face of it, big progress in the course of the war. The Axis powers in Northern Africa surrendered. The Allies invaded Sicily, Mussolini fell from power, and Italy signed an armistice as Allied forces landed on the mainland. But the Allies had to wage bitter battles against strong German defenses before they could launch the invasion of Normandy the following year and begin to free Europe. In 1943 the Allied navies and air forces gained ground on the sea and in intense bombing attacks on Germany.

In the summer of 1943 there were armed revolts by Jews in several ghettos across Eastern Europe, but, as I learned nearly fifty years later, it was on July 8, just a year after that last letter, that my family was being deported to Terezin and, only two months later, to Auschwitz. The killing of the Jews, the Nazi "Final Solution," was speeding up.

But whatever was known by the British government about the plight of the Jews in wartime was not, as far as I knew (but what did I know?), passed on to the British public, which was busy coping with heavy bombing, with the mobilization of all the men and women, young and not quite so young; those women not busy caring for small children were sent to work in munitions factories, onto the land to help with farming, or into the women's armed forces. There was a tragic loss of young life in the air and on the sea. There were many crises. Overall was an atmosphere of joint emergency and joint effort. The shortage of food, and many other everyday needs, like motor fuel and coal, prevented all but essential traveling, and life became very basic.

Many things had to be sacrificed to the "War Effort." People even gave up books they didn't need because there was such a shortage of paper; metal utensils, even iron railings, went toward making munitions to fight the enemy. No goods from overseas could reach Britain, of course; the sea was a war zone, and all Allied ships were used for battle. Domestic trains seemed always crammed with soldiers. The government's efforts to deal with all problems ruled our lives, and the people did indeed gear themselves up to a real spirit of determination to overcome these odds.

Seen from a child's perspective, a foreign child, I had hardly known a life free from crisis, so, as I was quite powerless amidst the events around me, I simply followed orders. Once my schooling had been decided and the shuttling between the Aunties had ceased, I settled to school in just the one town and progressed without trouble, at least in the primary school. Later I didn't do so well. Whether I was a late developer or didn't concentrate because of the traumas, I didn't work hard. Yet I wanted to study medicine. I don't understand this. I knew I had to earn a living soon but wasn't wise enough to study seriously and impress them with my diligence. Loans, grants, and part-time teenage jobs didn't exist. You went to university if your parents were able and willing to pay, otherwise you didn't go. Only a very few people, and I became one of them, were able to get into university under their own steam after the age of twenty-one. Only a small proportion stayed to take the Higher School Certificate and leave at seventeen, and less than 2 percent of the British population was university-educated, with few girls among them. When you left school at fifteen with your School Certificate, as I did, you worked full-time and supported yourself right away. School was the one place I could fool and giggle around, and they tolerated me, which was a very great pity.

It did take a little time to master the language; I learned words off the sides of buses. My spelling was phonetic for a while, like Czech. My means of expression were shaky. The Campbells had a cottage in the country where we went for weekends, and I liked "helping" the farmers round about. On one occasion I stepped into a fresh cowpat in a new pair of sandals. I cried bitterly, thinking I would be in trouble, "It was simply done!" I meant that the cow had only just dropped it. But as I learned English, I lost both my Czech and my German, never to regain them nor to have any facility in learning any other language but English.

My mother had introduced me to books: Little Red Riding Hood disappearing down the path into the wood. The sight of the Granny turning into a wolf. Snow White seen at the cinema was as bad. That awful witch, standing over the cauldron with her poisoned apple. Of course books give you another world, and quickly I was hooked, and still am. English books were like an ever-open sweetie shop. Doris had started me off with Beatrix Potter, since reading as an occupation for children was one of the few things of which she approved—some of the time; so I was very soon reading adult English books to myself. Two archaic specimens that gripped me very young were F. A. Anstey's *Vice Versa*, and *Mr. Midshipman Easy,* by "Captain Marriat," written in tiny print on thin, double-column paper. Mostly the books in the house were middlebrow, *Reader's Digest*–level, and I used the local library until it was exhausted. I wanted to read everything there was before I died.

But learning the language was the least of my problems. Relearning who or what I was and where I belonged was the main one, and that took about fifty years. For a very long time I minded not belonging anywhere, but not now. I'm on this globe with everyone else, and exactly where doesn't really signify in terms of self-worth. But it was a very big problem for many years. Was I Czech, was I English? Was I Jewish or Christian? We attended church at least once every Sunday, and I went to Sunday school as well and enjoyed it. At least I didn't feel disloyal to my parents in doing this; I knew they wouldn't have minded.

I tend to become more irritated nowadays when Orthodox Jews ask me, "How could you bear to be rescued by Christians?" I say, "If you're struggling in the water, will you argue with your rescuer?" Others lavish sympathy on me for having lost my Jewish heritage. This again is an alienating assumption, for this is one conflict I was spared, since I didn't have a religious heritage to lose, and by then the Christian one seemed to me as good as any other. Yet of course the loss of identity and feeling of belonging is there. I can't argue it away.

More to the point, where *were* the Jewish homes, and most particularly the Orthodox Jewish homes, when they were needed in 1939? Some Orthodox children lost their lives because such homes were in short supply, and their religious leaders refused to compromise with any other kind of home. I've learned recently that there simply were not enough offers, and the gap had to be filled by Christians. Of course the deficit can partly be explained by statistics—there were more Christian than Jewish homes in Britain; nevertheless it is a fact that, with the notable exceptions of B'nai Brith and Rabbis Shoenfeld, Landi, and some others, few rabbis seem to have led their congregations, by example and precept, to open their doors in welcome. It was even felt by some Jewish leaders that these Kindertransports should not be encouraged, as they might provoke more anti-Semitism. However, a number of Jews, poor as well as rich, did come forward in response to general appeals and take children in, and the outcome in terms of happiness, as in the Christian homes, was mixed.

My foster father's behavior was extraordinary. When I received a menorah—a Jewish ritual candelabrum, whose meaning was unknown to me—from one of my mother's English friends, he repeatedly wished me happy Hanukkah as a big joke. He also made fun of the Czech national anthem by chortling its title, "Where Is My Home?" When he beheld anyone different from himself, he loved to say, speaking behind his hand like a comedian, again as a big joke, "A foreign gentleman" or "A Jew." I do believe he actually meant no harm. He was shy and didn't know how to relate to people. I believe he actually liked me, and these jokes were his form of friendship.

I had arrived in a strange home. It didn't mesh with the rest of the world, and its outlook was hostile, suspicious, and patronizing. Class and position were paramount. Doris had stepped up in the world, yet trade, from which Arthur's family made its money, was also despised. So the position was anomalous, and I was always conscious of it. Doris's in-laws despised her for her poor manners, and they lived "bigger" than her family, so that was enough to make them superior. Arthur was the indulged eldest and only son; he had three sisters, none of whom was educated seriously. This was normal, as education in middle-middle England was barely considered worthwhile for women. If they managed to find a husband, which was by no means certain, since the loss of young men in the First World War had made this a problem, and the current war was repeating it, then marriage was considered a full-time career. And if they didn't, there was enough money in this family for each girl to become a "lady" (or spinster, as unmarried women were disparagingly called) "of independent means."

Leisure was the most prized attribute in England at that time, denoting financial and social superiority, a favor bestowed by God, marking and rewarding your worth. Those who did have to work were both used and despised. The professions, of course, were exempt from this view, except among the aristocracy, who saw doctors as only slightly above tradesmen. People were measured from this perspective, and this state of their world was seen as permanent, immutable, and, above all, right. Those who felt their own superiority were brazen in its display.

There was one other sign, besides leisure, enabling everyone to place everyone else on the social scale, and that was speech. Everyone developed the most finely tuned ear. It didn't take me long to acquire it. Every tiny sound and nuance, inflection, specific word or expression used, told the world where you came from (which was very important) and what and who you were. I once asked Harry, the Campbells' eldest boy, why his parents had spent money on private schools for me when I might have done better at a state grammar school, and he said it was because it would have embarrassed them if I had picked up a bad accent at a free, state school.

You were judged not by what you had achieved but by who your father was. That is, if he was in a low position, so were you. You were expected to stay in the station to which you had been born. We even sang hymns saying so:

The rich man in his castle,
The poor man at his gate,
He made them High or Lowly,
And ordered their estate.
All things Bright and Beautiful,
The Lord God made them All!

This is what Doris meant when she told me later that I "didn't know my place," meaning that I should be servile in my attitude because my parents would have been her servants. I made haste to copy the speech of my ladylike teachers and not Doris's South London, for, interestingly enough, Doris did not speak or act like a lady. To speak like a lady (though you would never fool the aristocracy, who made special sounds and words of their own, and, besides, all knew one another) was as important as education. In fact, you could get education if you were lucky, but if you didn't speak right, your chance of a professional job was nil. You didn't even get admitted to study for it.

I could feel no fun or laughter in the home; the atmosphere made me tiptoe. Nobody seemed to relax or do anything together, especially not talk. It was a house, not a home. A base from which to go out and do the interesting things. Arthur's and Doris's marriage seemed a bit formal and unreal, and although she knew she'd done well by it, she was very conscious of her financial dependence and social inferiority compared to her in-laws. A part of her discontent and aggression may have come from this. She was another woman who had wanted an education and been denied it.

Arthur tended to placate her—"Yes, yes, my dear"—and absent himself in work and hobbies. He was out most evenings, either at committee meetings, where, she said, "He loves to throw his weight about," or at theater song practice. They liked amateur theatricals, men dressing up as women, Gilbert and Sullivan. She too was often out at meetings for the Red Cross, hobbies, and crafts, but I heard nothing about Girl Guides anymore. She also liked public speaking and would give talks to church or women's groups on any subject whatsoever.

As Aunt Zdena had remarked, the Campbells' house was huge. It stood on a corner with its own overhanging sweet chestnut tree. They'd had it built in the late twenties, and I know now that it was a wonderful period piece. The furnishings, wallpapers, and curtains were pure thirties, with the oranges, green, medium blue, and cream colors popular at the time, and I loved the angular art deco shapes in the patterns. I was obsessively interested in decoration and would study all this, and plan future rooms of my own. Doris had dozens of flower vases, of every shape and kind, and allowed me to fill them with flowers from both her gardens and decorate each room with one of these arrangements.

The ground floor was filled with a central hall, a big drawing room to the right as one entered, and a downstairs cloakroom. To the left was the medical suite—a waiting room and consulting room—and the patients entered by the side door.

Behind that was the accommodation that my parents and I would have lived in. A fairly dark kitchen at the back, with a door giving on to the rear garden; a biggish but rather dark sitting room at the right as one entered the flat, overlooking a dank Victorian side garden, with drooping ferns and a stagnant sunless pond in the corner. The bedroom was to the left of the side door as one entered that way. This was lighter. There were pantries and larders, and under-stair nooks and crannies, with more stairs leading to the cellar.

This was filled with ammunition for Arthur's hobby of shooting. We were later sheltering, during air raids, over this cache of guns and bullets. He was a member of the Home Guard—a force composed chiefly of elderly or slightly infirm men, regarded with some affectionate derision by the populace—which intended to defend Britain in case of invasion. He and other veterans of the previous war relived old glories and practiced for new ones, rustling around among our garden bushes. They are immortalized in the apparently accurate and still wonderfully funny TV series *Dad's Army.*

A wide oak staircase to the next floor, and I would sit at the top of this when I was very young, reading Rupert books, my ears twitching for trouble. Where *are* you? Are you *reading?* (A crime when I should be doing chores.) There was orange angular patterned wallpaper in the large casement-windowed dining room, each window with its own little frilled net curtain fastened on brass rods top and bottom. A big mahogany dining table in the center, and across the landing their blue-and-cream bedroom, with a little sitting room for Doris in between.

Here was where she read to me at the beginning. It was a charming room, with small inlaid mahogany reproduction Regency blue-and-cream covered chairs, and a balcony over the chestnut tree and the quiet road. She kept a small cylinder filled with "thruppeny" bits," and I actually dared take one of these from time to time. Had she noticed, the trouble would have been terrible. I remember thinking, as I stole one of these, that I didn't know why I was doing it.

Next to the dining room was a big bedroom for me. This was nice; it was big enough for me to turn cartwheels in. When I wasn't reading, I was standing on my head; headstands, handstands, one-armed cartwheels, I was the expert. And James, the younger boy, would play cricket with me. There was a plug in the wall, connected to the only radio in the house (known as the wireless), in the next-door dining room. On no account must I listen to this without permission. On one occasion Doris was convinced I had done so while she and Arthur were out in the evening, because the sound came on automatically at breakfast in the morning. They would dress up in evening clothes to go to the theater, Doris in a long dress, Arthur in dinner jacket, and my job was to clear their early-supper things, lay the breakfast, and put myself to bed at six. My denials were fruitless; I was punished with silence for three days. I didn't own a radio myself until I was given one as a twenty-first-birthday present.

Along the corridor was, I think, the only bathroom in the house (I don't know if there was one in what would have been "our" flat, downstairs). At night one was expected to use the china chamber pot under the bed, not to go to the lavatory next to the bathroom. These pots had thirties patterns on them, too, and are now collector's items. Mine had blue and yellow irises. It was someone's job to empty them each morning. Why were we not using the lavatory? Doris was bowel-obsessed. Jane told me recently that if she didn't "go" for three days, she was smacked. I was threatened with an enema at the end of the week, so learned to exaggerate. As for sex, in a doctor's house we all knew how babies were born, but how did they get there? No one let on. But I had my books. Doris wanted to make sure to spoil sex, so she told me, "You needn't imagine it's all fun. It hurts like hell, and you bleed like a pig." I didn't believe her, but it frightened me all the same.

Along this corridor, beyond the bathroom, was another big spare bedroom and, at the end, a small, ugly, inconvenient kitchen painted a horrible dark green, with a high, dusty, viewless little window that let in only a hazy light. Next to the kitchen there was a tiny scullery with porcelain sink and wooden draining board for washing up, and a larder/store cupboard.

Up the stairs to the attic, and two more big spare rooms with windows in the eaves and a lot of charm. And lots of box rooms for trunks, sports equipment, and so on. Jane and I, or any visitor, would gossip up here, but we were soon found, and I would be given jobs to do.

Arthur and Doris were both used to being waited on, and I never saw Doris do what I would call work. That is, cook, clean, or even wash up. Washing and ironing, making beds, gardening—everything was done by others, but she did supervise quite a lot, and taught me how to bottle fruit, make jam, and cook a few dishes, and I was happy to learn these things.

Shopping was a ritual on which I had to accompany her during school holidays. She would always drive, and I think it was on Mondays. Each shop was small and traditional, and service was personal, given by the owner. Boxes of biscuits were displayed below and along the front of the counter; everything was weighed and measured, usually in very small quantities, like half or a quarter of a pound, and wrapped into square packets with darkly colored paper, like a kind of cheap drawing paper, each color according to the contents. Blue for sugar, red for sultanas, and so on. My husband tells me that these colors were standardized; they were the same at his local grocer's. Each tradesperson was a character, always called "Mr." and then his full surname, and fixed in one's mind like an institution. The bacon-slicing chart and machine were fascinating, showing the minutest grades of thickness that you could choose. The wrapping interested me, because in Prague the food had been wrapped into conical shapes.

I squirmed to see the grocer, butcher, or greengrocer fawn on Doris, bowing and scraping. Yes, Mrs. Campbell. No, Mrs. Campbell. She would tell family news in front of other customers, embarrassing me even more. Then she would not take the goods home herself. They would be delivered by an errand boy on a bicycle, which had a large flat iron carrier on the front. And everything would be delivered to the back-door tradesmen's entrance; they never entered by the front.

Then, on Fridays, the other end of the ritual. We drove around to Pay the Books. Each tradesman filled in a column in his own book, listing what she had bought, with the invoice at the bottom. So we would go and pay these in person. Sometimes she would order for the next week, explaining who was visiting her. Alcohol never passed anyone's lips. All her family had signed The Pledge when young, and stuck to their promise not to drink, all their lives.

Visiting the dress shop was quite entertaining. "Modom" would try on several dresses in a big changing room with a full-length tilting mirror while I sat in a small frilled chair facing her, and the saleswoman stood attentive, ready to admire or make an adjustment. Doris often asked my opinion. She would then have her selections packed in boxes and tissue and sent, never taken, home "on appro." Afterward, anything she didn't want was collected and taken back to the shop. She had a lot of good clothes in spite of clothes rationing: fine, well-cut, detailed wool for winter, and bright flowered silk crepe and cotton for summer. Her shoes were fine leather, in elegant styles and with high heels. Doris loved clothes, but there was a saying in the family, handed down from her mother: "Who do you think is going to look at *you?*" Vanity was, naturally, a sin. So she bought clothes in defiance. In spite of the war, clothes were still beautiful in those days. I admired the handmade silk underwear in shop windows. Doris made sure that her family had the minimum essentials, and I often got Jane's castoffs, but in wartime that was normal.

Deodorants were not in general use, and people smelled, especially the men, whose suits were heavy and seldom cleaned. There was a shortage of hot water, due to lack of fuel. People bathed once a week. Some houses still had no bathroom, and some had lavatories outside. Even grand houses were damp and cold, without central heating. Gas, coal, or electric heaters, just one in each room, in the fireplace, burned our knees and froze our backs. All the heat went up the chimney. The British had all sorts of notions of superiority to other nations, including cleanliness, but they were more backward than they knew.

I seldom remember Doris walking—it's funny how some people just seem made for wheels, and she was most unusually lucky in having a car of her own. Very few housewives at that time did. She and Arthur gained all sorts of privileges for themselves, for petrol because he was a doctor and made house calls, and to produce food in the country. I just don't know where all this food went. There was no need for anyone to be hungry. There were hens and ducks for eggs and meat, goats for milk, rabbits, honey, vegetables, and fruit. Even walnuts and chestnuts from their own trees, and sugar to give to the bees. But there was never enough to eat, especially for children. Not even for her own children.

But perhaps she would walk to church, or to exercise the dogs. She even enjoyed warfare on their behalf. There was a particular chow whose house we had to pass on the way to church. I dreaded this and begged to go another way to avoid a fight. The chow and one of our dogs knew and despised each other, and a tumult would ensue as Doris let them fight it out. Her theory was that the chow's owners had no right to let him roam loose, and no one was going to stop *her* from walking down their street.

She managed to employ servants even during the war, usually people too infirm to go into the armed services. They provided character and a sideshow all their own. One in particular impressed us all. She had a glass eye; her eye had been removed. One day she had been frying bacon, and *splat,* the fat went into her eye, and she lost the sight. After hearing about that, we all made sure to wear glasses to fry bacon. Arthur, of course, was unaware of housework. I never saw him enter the kitchen when I was young, pick up a plate from the table, hold a hammer, or even look at the garden. His only job was to carve the small roast of meat on Sundays, when it was hot, and on Mondays, when it was cold. After that it became Shepherd's Pie. The meat ration was very small, and he excelled at cutting tiny transparent slices with jokes about overeating. Sometimes we did have a chicken or rabbit from the country. The majority of people at that time were slim.

Mealtimes were a bad time of tension. Anything could happen. In spite of her constant talk, I didn't know what either she or Arthur was thinking. They must have made certain decisions about me privately, for she would relay information by saying, "We have decided . . . " and then tell me what I had to do.

At the Christian church, no one would have dreamed of saying, "What is this Jewish child doing here?" They didn't differentiate such subtleties. It didn't occur to them to wonder if it might be disturbing my religious orientation to be taught to worship in a Christian church. At school it was the same. I joined in all the worship without question, although the headmistress knew my background. She told Doris she had noticed that Jewish children always seemed interested in religion.

The local Jewish committee must have sent round one of its inspectors from time to time, but I never dreamed that there might be other refugees locally. Her visits were despised and resented, and when she came, Arthur was at his most humorous, insisting on taking her to see the lavatory and telling her, "You see, we do have proper lavatory paper here!" Of course she didn't ask me any questions, and I knew very well I could be sent somewhere worse.

Should I be adapting to being in England permanently, or should I be ready to return to Prague if my parents survived? Would they survive? How would I adapt back after six or more years? This was never discussed, by anyone, ever. What was I supposed to do with it? The difference between my adoptive culture and the one I'd left behind was so profound that I couldn't carry both. I had to decide between the two. Naturally I had to choose the one on the spot. There was no way I could have hung on to being Czech or Jewish. I would have been laughed to scorn. But, of course, to Czechs I was a traitor, because to them the British were funny and foreign, too, and I should have stuck to my origins.

It was alienating and very lonely. Worst of all was the absence of my loving, accepting parents. I doubt if a day has passed in my life when I don't think of them. This can't be usual among people who've led a normal life, surely? Of course nobody *ever* asked me if I was missing them. It was as if they had ceased to exist. At this point we didn't know if they had or not, but in my mind and need they remained for good.

Doris was a big dominating figure, tall, not thin, with a loud voice, very frightening to me; she came from a family which dominated. When asserting herself, she would take a deep breath, throw out her chest like a pouter pigeon, and lift her chin in challenge. Only her younger son, and her even more dominating eldest brother, could cope. The rest of her world she vanquished. Mostly she socialized with her brothers and sisters and the rest of her own family. Only the family was invited for meals, except sometimes on Sundays, when American soldiers billeted in the area who had attended the church service might be offered lunch. They were very sweet and would push a candy bar across the table to me.

Interaction with her was a one-way street. She talked; others listened and responded to orders. We never did have a conversation in all the years I knew her. She didn't listen, and she never asked questions except about domestic tasks done or not done. I had complete privacy in my head. She never asked me what I had done at school or anywhere else. She had no idea who my friends were. I was a nuisance, even though she had invited me and insisted on keeping me when she knew my parents couldn't reach England. She knew that my mother's friend Elsie wanted me, and she certainly wasn't going to give in to *her.* Yet when I think about it, she got quite good service from me. She taught me to massage her back, place damp cloths on her head for her migraine, and hold her head when she was sick. And of course I had many domestic tasks, was a good listener, and didn't argue. Her highest compliment was, occasionally, that I had been "useful."

She preferred animals to people and told this to the world, and particularly to me. "Don't you dare ill treat my animals!" when I had knocked accidentally against her bird's cage. "We chose to have them. You were pushed onto us." We all knew this to be untrue, yet she would say such things in front of others. She didn't know shame. I think this brought me to my lowest ebb. She said it after we'd learned the fate of my parents, just before I returned to visit Prague in 1947, when I was fifteen.

I began to wonder if I really existed, or should exist. I can remember walking about in a sort of vaporous cloud of misery. Because of her dislike of child rearing, she had left the upbringing of her own children to nannies and boarding schools. And then she landed herself with me, instead of gaining two servants.

She managed to tolerate me while I was very young, even teaching me a few skills when I became a Brownie, of course! And she did take the trouble to teach me conventional good behavior, always writing to thank people for presents, and so on. But her tirades if crossed were fearsome, and quite often she made false accusations.

She did have one and a half friends; Arthur had none.

The half-friend was really a friendly acquaintance, the wife of one of Arthur's partners. I lived with her for one week while Doris and Arthur went on holiday, and it was a revelation. I had enough to eat, and this tall lady, who was warm and smiling, saw me off at the garden gate each morning when I went to school and actually wished me a happy day!

The other, pretty well a real friend, was a sweet woman. Mother and daughter together, both widows. War had dispatched at least one of their husbands. These two lived nearby in the upper half of a house, which was filled with Victorian furniture and ornaments. And now I remember, some art nouveau vases, too. Mrs. Etheldene had a lovely smile on a very white face; she would open the glass porch door to me without saying a word; I would pass the ferns and possibly aspidistras in the hall, and we would go upstairs, and I knew I was welcome.

I visited her fairly often, delivering errands or messages. The phone was not used frivolously, and I think Mrs. Etheldene didn't have one, so messages were always taken on foot. She had time for me, and although I can't remember what we talked about, we would sit in front of her gas fire, which went *pop pop pop,* and her small round copper kettle, resting on a hob on the dark green tiles in front of her fireplace, sizzled as it boiled. And we would have a cup of tea, always in fine pretty china cups. No one I ever met had anything but good china. You had to be starving poor not to have that. The windows were swathed in cream lace curtains, and of course the sofa was dark green velvet.

They seemed very poor in that respectable genteel way which was often called "as poor as a church mouse" and looked as if they didn't get enough to eat, but she was gentle and nice and had a wry sense of humor. It sounds so traditional as to be a caricature, but many widows and spinsters lived exactly like that. They didn't go out to work, they had no profession or skills, and scraping by on a tiny pension and "looking after the house" seemed a normal way of life. If you were even poorer than that and couldn't afford rent, the only job for a lady was either as a companion for a rich old widow or as a governess. The normal widows' pensions were tiny, and so were wages, even in many professional jobs. Mrs. Etheldene's father, like Doris's, had been a pastor, so they were called "daughters of the manse." She told me that when she went anywhere with Doris, she felt like the ladies' maid, but she said it with tolerant humor, and even Doris was fond of her.

We kept in touch until she died in her nineties, and when I was middle-aged she told me she had loved me on sight when she met me after I arrived in England, but, typically for the day, she had never openly showed it, and I'd been quite unaware of it.

I think I knew that I had entered a past age; Arthur, Doris, and her friends were ten years older than my parents, and he was seven years her senior, but I found it interesting and felt it expanded my understanding to hear stories of the olden days. An atmosphere of sin and punishment did seem to haunt their backgrounds. I suppose I must have caught the tail end of the Victorian era. The old people, and old age began at about forty, didn't so much wear dresses as swathe themselves, usually in gray, black, or purple. And they acted feeble and dominated the young.

The burgeoning of an intelligent person was too much for Doris. I asked her sister Kathleen some years later why Doris had treated me as she did, and she replied, "She wanted to break you." She came near to succeeding, and I feel that only my genes and earlier care got me through. I felt as if she had continued with the mental annihilation where Hitler finished with the physical. However, here I am, healthy today. This all happened a long time ago, and I have long since forgiven her. She was as she was and simply took on a job for which she was unfitted. How do I know I could have done much better?

Her sister Kathleen was religious, a missionary abroad among the heathen. She was small and frail and loved to boast that when she went into the bush with the natives they took a tape measure, the better to fit the latrine seat to her tiny bottom. She certainly tried to convert me to Christianity, but I didn't mind. I appreciated her interest. And I must say that a certain feeling I have of the "reality" of God, even if intermittent, even if more a hope than a sure belief, came from her teaching. But I see God as all-denominational. Jesus didn't make such an impact—or perhaps that's my Jewishness manifesting! Kathleen told me she would love to be Jewish, because Jesus was a Jew. In fact, she was sincere in her wish to unite Christians and Jews in friendship and was a board member of the Society for Christians and Jews. For a time, she introduced me to the evangelical branch of the Christian faith, and I hoped it might make me feel better, because, she told me, God loved us all. Unfortunately, He did not get through to me when I needed Him most, and I find it rather worrying that God should seem more real to me when I feel well.

She was benevolent, though there was that strange sadistic undertow, the punishing Victorianism, with which they'd all been brought up. Their mother lived for the church and saw sin everywhere. For instance, when Kathleen explained to me that her sister had wanted to break me, she said it with a certain relish, as if breaking people was quite an acceptable and recognized way of exerting power. Also, quite oblivious to the hurt it might cause, she quoted her mother as saying of me, "We don't know where she came from."

Kathleen was single and kept an interested eye on all her nieces and nephews, and was ready to step in and help whenever she saw a need. I enjoyed gossiping with her and was grateful for any help but maintained a certain wariness. Her left hand didn't entirely know what her right hand was doing. I miss her now she is dead. She was the family link and newsletter.

The kindness that I did receive from Kathleen and my foster siblings tended to feel like kindness shown to an unfortunate outsider, not one of their own. That was actually true and couldn't be helped, but it was made worse by the gradual development of my own warped perception of myself. The family knew Doris well, and years later, a cousin told me that whenever I was mentioned, people would say, "That poor little Milena, she's turned her into a servant."

Doris's daughter Jane and I became friends and even co-conspirators. We'd go walking in the country, downhill through the cowslip field behind the cottage and into the bluebell wood at the bottom. It was very beautiful with its peacefulness, its rustling branches and sunny clearings. I'd go there alone sometimes, and no one worried about safety. Jane and I would swap indignation at outrages suffered, and plot revenge. Although conspiracy was better than nothing, it was rather bleak comfort. She and her brothers were adult now and lived away from home. Harry was studying medicine in London, and therefore safely exempt from military service, and she was working as a nurse at the local hospital.

But earlier, in the winter of 1943, when I was eleven, I came to breakfast one morning, and Arthur was sitting in his big mahogany chair at the head of the table; his face was strange. Doris was at the table beside him, the copper coffee warmer next to her. On its flat top sat the aluminum percolator in which the coffee had actually boiled, kept warm by a small candle. She was crying, which was not unusual. She often cried with self-pity and to get her own way, but this time there was a different reason.

"James is missing in the North Sea," she said. James was their second and favorite son. He was twenty-one. They'd received one of those telegrams.

From my own point of view, this was an added sadness, although I remember the feeling as another blank. I didn't seem to know how to react anymore. All deaths somehow felt as if they were expected. I've had this reaction to death ever since. He had been extra kind to me. He was a jolly boy, everyone's favorite. I have a nice picture of him in his baggy trousers, holding my hand, and I am smiling. And on my wall at home is a lovely white plaster bas-relief of his head, life-size, made when he was two years old.

Jane and I had a lot of laughs, but we were very different. She had a good attitude toward disagreement; she'd say, "We'll agree to differ." We never quarreled, and I've always appreciated her generosity. She too was forced to leave school early, without even taking her school leaving exams. She really wanted to work with animals but somehow found herself cornered into nursing. Despite feeling childish and low in self-esteem, she nevertheless had a sense of belonging and family pride.

And despite our longstanding friendship, I've never talked to her about my own family. I feel she would share the general attitude that looking back is futile and insulting, and she's never asked me any questions whatsoever. It's as if my whole background never existed. It was unimportant.

The war was a nightmare even in unoccupied England, saved by that tiny stretch of water, the English Channel, plus the determination of the people, led by Winston Churchill, to fight and win. This gave the country a unique quality, almost innocence; the people did not know oppression. That period is now bound in myth and legend, and the expression "Britain's Finest Hour" that attaches to it is not so ludicrous. We even watched the Battle of Britain, fought over our heads in sunny autumn daylight, in 1940 as we picked blackberries in the hedgerows in the country; small planes curling high, Ours and Theirs, and then a puff of white plume as one hurtled to the ground. I think it was this intense feeling of togetherness, Us against the Enemy, that knitted the people so strongly together and gave them that belonging feeling that I was missing.

Yet I was taking part in it, too, and did feel it to an extent. The countryside was beautiful, its scenery, gardens, and flowers—every wildflower known by name—lovely and loved by all, including me. I grew to love the British in spite of everything. Even with their prejudices and truly awful class system, many were lovable, and above all they were extremely funny, both deliberately and unintentionally. I loved the fact that laughter was and is a huge part of British life. The nice, not snobbish, British have a coziness to their personalities that I haven't met elsewhere. Their sense of drama was fully fed at this time. I think things did not get truly depressing until after the war, when, without the drama and challenge and with continuing material deprivations, life just became dreary. It was anticlimax.

Every night we ran to the shelter while the bombs thumped down. Doris was not at all afraid. Her own spirit was warlike, she was in her element. And I don't remember feeling fear of the bombs myself. Our shelter was the metal type you had indoors, known as a Morrison. The outdoor one you put in your garden, in a sort of home-dug bunker, was an Anderson. Our Morrison stood in the middle of the square hall downstairs, like a very strong chicken coop, with metal mesh sides and very solid top which should resist the pressure when the house fell on top of you. There was room for an entire family in it, lying down.

Arthur ran outside to watch the planes as soon as the air raid warning sounded. The warning was an absolutely unforgettable, sinister, breath-stopping wail. Up and down, *whooo oooh.* So was the sound of enemy aircraft, heavy, very low and slow, quite different from a British plane. Arthur never entered the shelter, mindful, perhaps, of the ammunition beneath. Doris and I did, but where was the maid? I don't ever remember a maid in the shelter. Was she under the stairs, which was considered another relatively safe place? Doris kept a tin of charcoal biscuits in the Morrison, black oblong things, astringent and powdery on the teeth. Fascinating in a revolting sort of way.

All sugar was in very short supply, and we resorted to strange foods to compensate. She allowed me to cook, and I made peppermint lumps of dried milk, water, and peppermint essence. I craved sugar, and the sweet allowance each week was about six to ten Smarties, half an ounce, that is two ounces a month altogether. I would count these out on the floor; the favorite colors, brown and black, chosen first, the color licked off, the inside inspected and maybe shown for admiration to anyone who was interested, and then gradually allowed to melt on the tongue.

But in spite of the food from the cottage garden, I was always hungry. Doris didn't believe in feeding children anything after their four o'clock tea—this consisted of two small triangles of thin bread, a scrape of margarine *or* a very little jam on the second piece only, and a mug of milk—until breakfast the next day. And that continued almost until one left home, and applied to her own children too. The food I ate was counted, and I was told how much it cost. Doris had a special thing about tomatoes, which were costed to include the gardener's wages.

When I eventually left home at sixteen to do nursing, I immediately earned a tiny sum, was clothed in uniform, fed (extremely meagerly), and housed. Most of the girls looked forward to visiting their homes during their short times off. I would go, too, sometimes, still looking for a feeling of home. One day at the end of such a visit, my friend Esmé came to meet me so we could walk back to the hospital together, and as I left, she heard me being charged sixpence for the kipper I'd eaten, since I should have eaten at the hospital, where the food was included as part of my pay. I grew reluctant to take food from Doris, and it became part of that feeling of wondering if I were alive. Doris was devastated by the loss of her son, and I felt deep pity for her. It overshadowed both her life and Arthur's, and though I knew I could not compensate for him, I did wish she could have enjoyed me just a little bit. Sometimes I felt that my own presence added to her resentment.

I wanted to be a good daughter to her, but she was unable to let me. Not being allowed to love is as bad as not being loved, and I was deprived of both. I was made to leave school at fifteen, because it was too expensive to support me at a private school, and then to take a year's domestic science course until I left home at sixteen. I continued to visit and keep in touch until she died in her late eighties, always hoping she would show some warmth or interest. But she couldn't. I had a fantasy, as a child, of coming home from school and both of us sitting on either side of the fire, myself wearing slippers, and talking, really talking. But it never happened. Poor Doris; her foul behavior was a misguided search for love, and she never knew she missed it by a hair's breadth.

In spite of everything, I felt I owed her courtesy, for she had, after all, given me house room and saved my life. I also knew I must never behave as she did. The unusual thing about her was that she didn't mind being hated by the people she overcame and never realized that she was depriving herself of good relationships. She had a wonderfully brazen childishness and would say, for example, as she took the only piece of citrus fruit available, "My mother always served herself last and gave herself the worst, but I'm making sure I *never* do that."

By this time I had lost almost every bit of self-esteem I had arrived with. Or rather, I was thrown into confusion. Was I as good as my parents felt, or as bad as Doris said? I suspected it was the former, but it would take fifty years before I was fully convinced. I lived in an atmosphere that told me I was a bad person, a disgrace. I have absolutely no idea what that disgrace was about, but since the tiniest domestic infraction was a crime, that may have been enough. On one occasion, the receptionist downstairs, in the job my mother would have held, used one sheet of paper too many to write professional messages. Or perhaps even used this sheet for her own purposes. That was a crime and a disgrace, too. This general disapproval quickly extended to anyone who spent more than a day in that house.

Doris actually wished me to fail and forecast my downfall daily. Despite evidence to the contrary. "You'll never pass your exams, you have no friends, you can't achieve anything, you have no money, have you?" Also, no one would ever want to marry me, what with my Jewish looks and my general badness. Whenever I passed my exams, she hated to know. She never learned what my eventual profession was. She couldn't bear anyone to have any success she had not had herself. This extended to her own daughter, but not to her two sons.

To this day I don't know what my crime was, except that I existed. She would say, "What cheek!" if anyone expressed any need, or asserted rights. I certainly did nothing to rebel, as such a concept hadn't yet arrived in Britain, and I was very afraid. At most, I might venture denial of a false accusation. Sometimes my housework wasn't quite perfect, but that amounted to, say, not hanging a tea towel straight on the rail. It was a mystery. A pure destructive process.

I would think of my mother and grieve at what she would have made of my misery, after all her efforts to save me. I was told, "You don't know your place" (meaning in the servants' quarters), "You don't realize what luxury you're living in," and "You need discipline." Sometimes she would feel poor and say, "You don't think I'm going to do without luxuries to feed *you,* do you?" Yet an interesting aspect to all this hatred is that I do believe it isn't as bad as indifference, because the person is still engaged with you enough to find you worth hating. When later on I discovered indifference, which was quite a new and striking concept to me, I realized that the level of rejection inherent in indifference is far greater and even more damaging. This was borne out when I talked with my fellow refugees. To be subjected to indifference was killing to the spirit.

The British were very anti-Semitic, in the sense that they regarded Jews as somehow dirty. *All* foreigners were funny, both ha-ha *and* peculiar funny, but the Jews were beyond funny—they were definitely not nice. This was clearly conveyed to me by most adults, but not by the children. Never once did I meet any form of ill treatment from the children at any school I went to, nor from the teachers. They behaved like ladies, and I realized I must emulate them and not the behavior I was seeing at home.

But feeling beyond the pale in being Jewish went very deep. It made me so fearful of danger and ostracism that I hide it among ignorant people to this day. I don't think, though I'm not quite sure, that I actually expected to be rounded up and killed. Just whispered about and regarded as dirty and inferior. The subject of Jews was almost taboo in society and in the newspapers. The implication was that they had *almost* brought all their troubles upon themselves.

Apart from her dreadful loss, Doris flourished during the war. She was active in volunteer work and loved excitement and emergencies. Arthur went doggedly on with his practice. He took pride in it and enjoyed it, and he was kind to his patients, which I respected. It would have been nice if he could have defended me against Doris, but I understood why he didn't dare.

Some of his family were uneducated snobs. His widowed mother and two unmarried sisters were idle except for a little church work or hobbies. They were openly patronizing and anti-Semitic and treated me like a charity case. When I got married, one of them asked me, "Does his family mind that you are Jewish?"

This was the scene then, when war ended. I had dealt with my situation by becoming extremely introspective. I thought through all my problems on my own, and I vowed I would be healthy and have a decent career one day. I knew I was battling for mental health daily. I can remember my desperate determination as if it were today. All my physical and mental strength went into it. Yet I was somehow aware that these miserable experiences could strengthen me in the long run if I used them right. But I also knew I would need some outside help to get me through, so for the moment I read psychology books, trying to understand myself and to cope, until I could find it.

It was particularly hard, the knowledge that Doris wanted me to fail. It was like climbing a slippery slope with a huge rock on my head. She had an expression, "I'll dance on your grave!" meaning "I'll gloat if you fail." She would gleefully say this in all sorts of situations about all sorts of people. One learned never to let on if one was happy or sad. She'd stamp on the first, and gloat over the second.

Britain celebrated noisily after Victory in Europe was announced. Before that, we had had the breath-holding period of the Allied landings, with American soldiers assembling in our particular part of the land, before the brave invasion of France and the forging through Europe toward Liberation, and then the first discovery, by British soldiers, of Belsen concentration camp.

What they found was shown on the newsreels at the cinema, and I saw it, on my own, I believe. Piles of skeletons—I was beyond reacting. I think my own emotions were pretty numb by that time. Some weeks later, I don't know exactly when, Doris came to me and said, "I'm afraid your parents did not survive. The Germans put them into a room all together, and gassed them." I think she mentioned that some of them went to their deaths singing the Czech national anthem. So she did allow me to preserve my respect for my parents, and she continued, always, to speak highly of my mother. I assume she got the information from my surviving relations. But that was the last time the subject was mentioned.

When we learned about my parents, I cannot say that I immediately started to grieve. But in a way, I had never stopped grieving. The first feeling I had, shameful as it sounds, was relief that I would not have to go back to Czechoslovakia and adapt to my original culture, which now felt foreign to me. This reaction was common among many Kindertransport refugees, I recently learned, but made me feel guilty at the time. I think I dreaded all the suffering I remembered, as manifested by the huddled elderly relations. I didn't then realize that there weren't any relations left to huddle, but I must have known instinctively that my parents would not have been the parents I had left behind, nor I the same child. But all this wasn't fully conscious.

The interesting thing was that no one, absolutely no one, asked me how I felt, and I didn't know either. Above all, when the numbness passed and I realized I was alone in the world, no one seemed to think for a moment that anything had happened to me at all. I was alive, wasn't I? I had a substitute family, didn't I? What impertinence, an insult, even, to grieve for anyone else. And the sad thing is, I *was* grateful. Shown just a bit of love and warmth, I'd have been a grateful puppy; it was all there, dammed up.

Then the isolation. I didn't know another person in the world to whom this had happened. Absurd as it sounds, I had come off one of those trains, one among 10,000, but had been too young to take in, or to remember later, that there were others who had literally been in the same boat. I had no idea until about 1988 that there *were* 10,000 of us. I had seen only one train and then forgot that there were other children on it, too, who had experienced the same things. I find this ignorance and forgetting unbelievable now.

About two years after the end of the war, the Campbells adopted me. I think Arthur must have suggested it, and I was told of their decision. I was not asked if I wanted it, but I didn't mind. They implied that this would greatly improve my chance of hiding my Jewishness, and I agreed with this view, never dreaming the trouble such a deception would cause me. One of Doris's brothers suggested I have my nose done, to hide the Jewishness still further. I didn't do this, but my feeling that my looks were inferior because of my nose remained for life.

The adoption was a peculiar thing for them to do, for they didn't allow me for one moment to feel that I belonged in the family. It can't have been easy for their grown children either, but they accepted it with good enough grace, if they were aware of it at all, for such things were not discussed. Maybe there was some affection on Arthur's part behind his odd behavior, but he could neither give nor receive warmth openly, and I was too immature—and I regret this and feel guilty for not trying harder—to cope with him and try to establish a relationship. Doris, I know, continued to feel that I wasn't nearly grateful enough.

5
The Outcome

We learned the end of the story of my parents, my aunts, Grannie, uncle, and three-year-old cousin fairly soon—a few months, I think—after the end of the war. My mother's cousin, Eva Roden, and her husband, Ruda, who were married at Terezin when Eva was sixteen, survived both Auschwitz and Belsen, and returned to Prague to tell the tale. I made a short visit there when I was fifteen. They took me to the top of a hill at Terezin, above Prague, and showed me the fields covered with small white crosses. They looked absolutely shattered after their experiences and told me quite a bit. I knew that I must know these things, but I was given an understanding of unspeakable suffering, torture, and killings; and again that visit was never questioned, or discussed by anyone.

Recently I've learned that this was the almost universal reaction to both refugees and camp survivors. Silence. No questions. It's not spoken of. I felt then, and still do, that if we had said anything, it would either have been disbelieved or regarded as an unhealthy, even indecent, dwelling either on irrelevance, or something that those who had provided a home would resent. In Britain, at least, it was part of the general custom of hiding all unpleasantness under the carpet. The stiff upper lip really did exist. It was socially unacceptable to blab, simply not done. Part of the social system. This may have prevailed everywhere, for camp survivors returning to their old homes all over Europe were met with the same deaf ears.

A few of the camp survivors had just one tiny advantage over me.

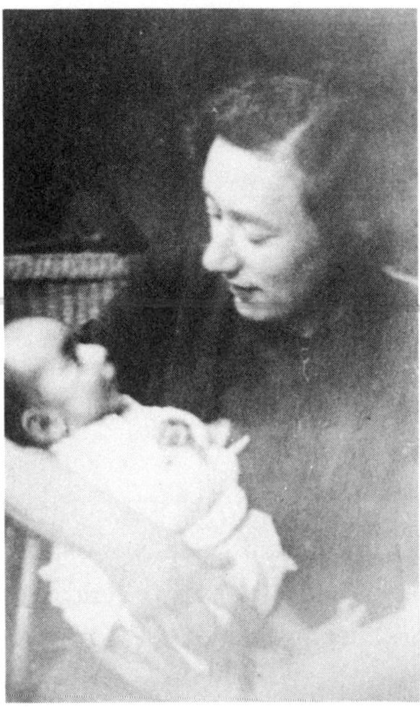

Milada Picková with baby Pavel, 1941.

They may have had fellow survivors they could speak to. But they may not have. I still didn't realize there were others like me. And, of course, in the face of these concentration camp atrocities, nothing had happened to me at all.

My own closest family were transported from Terezin to Auschwitz on September 8, 1943, and my information from the Prague Jewish Museum confirms this date. The museum even sent me details of their previous addresses and their transport numbers for both Terezin and Auschwitz; let no one say the Germans were careless in their killings. There was just one small discrepancy. The museum gives transport numbers to Terezin for my aunt Milada, her husband Arnošt, and their baby Pavel, but Eva says that Milada and the baby remained in Prague until the last deportation and went straight to Auschwitz, where they were killed immediately. They did not join the Czech family camp because immediate death was the normal fate for mothers with young children. But never mind small discrepancies; the fact is that they were murdered anyway. Eva and Ruda went to Auschwitz the following December. Eva writes in her section of *Lives on Borrowed Time,* the book she and Ruda wrote together:

> In 1943 the Germans established what they called a "family camp" at Auschwitz Birkenau. The first transport of five thousand people arrived there in September 1943 from Terezin, and nobody was gassed, not even the old, not even the sick, not even the children. On the contrary, they were all put into one camp; men and women in separate barracks, but still together.
>
> Our transport arrived in two sections at this camp, called B2B, on December 23rd, 1943, four thousand strong. We were also allowed to live. Everything was obviously done in preparation for some international inspection, which I cannot imagine, because we lived only two hundred yards away from the gas chambers. Whether the Germans hoped to barter us for medicine or some foodstuffs or whatever, I don't really know. But against all odds, we lived.
>
> The reality of the horror became clear to us within twenty four hours. We were only a small part of a huge compound in the surrounding camp of Auschwitz. The gassing went on and on around us. The ramp where the trains with the new arrivals stopped was just across the loaded barbed wire from us, and day and night we saw it all as clearly as a performance on a stage in front of us. We watched the arrivals, and the infamous Dr Mengele and his entourage conducting the selections. We saw the dogs barking, the S.S. men screaming and clubbing the new arrivals, and the senior inmates, the Capos, beating them; and then the flames shot high and the smoke was thick, and the dogs barked more viciously, and the camp orchestra played.

She continues for a page describing the conditions and how she and Ruda and her immediate family were, remarkably, still together, and how Ruda, who had been made head of the so-called medical barracks, was able to "organize" a little food and indoor jobs for his family. Eva worked in the children's barracks teaching the small children. She continues:

People were dying like flies, some from hunger or dysentery, some from beatings, some unable to stand for hours being counted. "Appel" [roll call] was held twice a day. Some just giving up. The ovens worked overtime; flames shot up high in the sky, and we thought we saw hell. But we did not; not yet. Because then came March 6th [*sic*] 1944. The friendly prisoners from the central registry office sent a messenger to our camp. "Beware, a big 'action' [*aktion*] (the [Germans'] term for the roundup and gassing of a large group without selection.) The Sondercommando is on duty." The Sondercommando was made up of prisoners who serviced the gas chambers and crematoria. They had very special privileges, but were periodically gassed with the victims, and a new commando was then formed.

Around noon, over blaring loudspeakers they ordered all the prisoners who had arrived from Terezin in September [my family's transport, which included Anna, Emil, Grannie, Lisa, and the rest] to come out from the barracks and stand in the usual rows of five to be counted, because they were going to be resettled in a completely new camp where they would work for a newly established industry, extremely important to the war effort of the Glorious Third Reich. Meanwhile, it was announced, all of them would be spending the night in the neighbouring camp B1B which had housed Russian prisoners until the day before but was empty now. And so they stood, men, women, and children. They did not quite believe what they were being told, but human nature being what it is, they hoped against hope. Some tried to hide, but they were found and beaten up and eventually forced to stand up while the Germans started to count again. Finally, maybe four or five hours later, when the count tallied, they were marched into the camp next to ours, but separated from us by double rows of loaded [electrified] wire.

We sat on our bunks and huddled together. The curfew was still enforced for us. Ruth [her friend] and I knew what would happen. But Mommy could not or would not grasp it. There was no appel for us that day and no food. There was by now only terror.

It started after dark. Truck after truck rolled into B1B and our friends [and my family, Anna, Emil, and the rest] were herded into them while the S.S. men kicked, clubbed, and screamed at them. Some of them went quietly, some pleading for mercy. Some tried to resist, and were shot on

> the spot, and then the dogs tore at the dead bodies, barking viciously. And some entered the trucks singing the Czech national anthem. Finally, towards dawn, the carnage was over; all was deadly quiet. As we watched through the tiny windows of the barracks, the red flames started to shoot up high and the black smoke poured from all the chimneys. All of the chimneys were working; everything was belching a hellish red and black towards the morning sky. I suppose we all died a little that night, but so strong was the will to live, to try to survive, in all of us, that the next day we went about our business as usual, and hardly dared to look towards the birches which hid the infernal ovens among them.

I think people who have lost loved ones will understand that I was thankful to have this information (the deaths are officially registered as being on March 8, 1944). It was something solid that I could grapple with. It gave me the assurance that their death was seen and marked at a specific time and place. One somehow needs to fix this in one's mind. Now that I have finally met others in the same boat, I find they agree, that they wish they knew the exact fate of their parents. All the Kindertransport refugees left when I did, during a ten-month period up to the outbreak of war on September 3, 1939, and some either never received letters again or never learned what happened, simply because not a single family member survived to tell them. A "disappearance" is even harder to come to terms with than these gruesome facts. Inasmuch as one can ever come to terms with such incomprehensible wickedness.

I realize when I look carefully through my mother's last letter and the letter from her best friend Heda (see chapter 6), describing their final days in Prague, that there is a gap during that year: I don't know at what point they left Grannie's house, where they were living with my aunt Míla's baby and the elderly relatives, and moved back to Prague. It may have been when they learned that the only way to postpone deportation was to work for the Jewish community in Prague, while the Jewish elders tried to bargain with the Germans. Or it may be that they were just turned out and forced to move to Prague 1, the district where all the Jews were being herded together into poor old apartments prior to deportation.

I wanted as full a picture of their lives as is available, both for myself and for writing this book, so I've been asking around lately, among distant or in-law cousins who survived the camps. Several mentioned that Míla was working at, or even running, a hospital. Eva had an idea that my mother may have been doing social work there with Míla. Eva herself worked with very young children, in Prague, Terezin, and even Auschwitz. She says the Germans were aware of the "secret" schools but turned a blind eye. But whether they were aware of the extent of the teaching, I don't know. Naturally the cousins were busy with their own problems at the time, all working in the Jewish community at anything that would bring them enough money to eat. They were also younger than my parents and would have seen them fleetingly if at all. Ruda thinks my father was working in a hospital for mental patients, later on, in Terezin. Of course, there are far bigger gaps in information than the one in the final year. If we didn't have Heda's letters, we would know very little about the time between my departure in '39 and the deportations in '43. But another cousin-in-law, Lida, who was deported and survived the camps, wrote me this little story:

> About your mother, Milena, yes, I do remember her, but it is a very short story and I do not know if I ever told it to anyone till recently. As a matter of fact, both your parents came once or twice to my parents house in Prague. It must have been in the first year after you went to England. They came to see me because we are the same age. I was born in May 1932 so you will be able to see if this part of my memory is right. [It is.] Your parents looked at me, your mother sat me on her knee and talked to me. But I was so shy, and the story of their little girl being alone, so far away from her parents, scared me so much, that this impression stayed with me all these years with the vision of your mother. I do remember your parents talking about you, in front of me, saying "Will she be this tall by now? Would she have long hair like this?" And such little remarks. I am sorry not to be able to add more. That is all there is to it. And as you see, there was in my mind no reason to upset you with my childish souvenirs when we met years ago.

So the consequence of all this was being left alone in the world, and is the hardest thing to write about, for the same reason that it was hard to talk about at the time or since. I write about it now, as best I can, not to indulge in morbid self-pity, which I certainly no longer feel, but to examine what it actually felt like and why it was so hard to deal with. I also want to explore other ways that have been found since then for dealing with such problems. You see how I write this preamble, because I still haven't recovered from the need to apologize for daring to "complain." We *were* saved, how dare we criticize anything? It goes very deep, and we're sensitive to criticism ourselves, because we lost our confidence in being allowed to have feelings or opinions at all.

Nowadays counseling help is brought in quickly in some instances of trauma, but this is a luxury that, I suspect, the recent victims of European and African atrocities have also been denied. In our case, as in some of theirs, we who were totally dispossessed were offered no help and had no group with which to identify either.

At that time and later, I think we colluded with the silence. We already felt different enough, and we didn't want pity—some of us had already had a lot of that. There's something patronizing about pity. It makes you feel weak and inferior. Loneliness is also a dread disease. It might be infectious, and it might imply a neediness that others can't handle or meet.

I had a natural bounce and sense of fun and covered my feelings to some extent. But one adult I worked with, a secretary, reproached me. "You behave as if you have the weight of the world on your shoulders." I reacted as I had learned to do over the years to all misunderstanding or insensitivities, with silence but with an inner rage and misery. It didn't occur to me to answer back, much less explain. I dared not act in any way that would make me stand out or provoke conflict by firmly stating my views. In other words, as far as I was concerned, assertiveness hadn't been invented. Aggression, yes, but that, whether given or received, threw me into more self-doubting confusion.

It was many years before I realized that I had a *right* to feel burdened. Auschwitz *was* the world's troubles. The enormity of it set me apart. I didn't have the innocence of the young people around me. And that was isolation enough to cause problems. I felt much older than they, and yet I'd missed the normal phase of lighthearted youth and was therefore in some ways immature at the same time. Isn't it extraordinary that the idea that there might be other people in the same situation as myself simply didn't occur to me? I believe it was because I was so busy trying to pretend to be British and normal that I couldn't think of Jewishness and refugeedom at the same time. I remember this quite clearly.

A Czech Jewish friend of the family, while I was first working in London after I'd finally been to university there, invited me to her North London home, was extremely kind and pleasant, and said, "Our home is your home." Yet I couldn't make use of it. At that time I could not cope with the multiple mixture that was myself. I had to stick with pretending to be British. Also, on reflection, is it possible to just graft oneself onto another home like that? Perhaps it requires confidence, which I didn't have at the time. No one wants to be another person's charity case.

How could I cross the chasm of nonunderstanding to express what it meant to be left truly alone? Or even to find out exactly how I did feel? The adults didn't want to hear—I really doubt if it even occurred to them. And my young contemporaries certainly couldn't imagine it; I didn't want to inflict my feelings on them or increase the gap between our experiences by talking about it. So it did become a collusive silence.

So how did it actually feel? I was encircled by bleak, empty space. I was a bad person. Doris had almost succeeded in convincing me, so I was vulnerable to everyone's opinion of my worth, defensive of any attack. Losing my whole family and background, my "right to exist," felt as if I had been cut off at the knees. There was a certain distance from the world: my experience felt different, my terms of reference didn't match other people's. If you have nobody, you do inhabit a different world. My friends would talk matter-of-factly about parents, family, events in which their people took part and of which they themselves were a part. There is an air of light cheerfulness as they talk. They have a sort of glow of being accepted in their circles. I had to guard my tongue lest all these differences showed. I mustn't stand out as different or to be pitied, or say anything that would actually make the space between us wider.

Years afterwards, I visited an old psychiatric colleague with whom I'd kept in touch. He commented on my current well-being and added, "You were a waif." So it had shown despite my efforts! And inside, of course, the space was there, and I felt bad, but I didn't know if it showed or was true. Even as I try to describe it, I realize my words are inadequate. It is so difficult to think myself back into that time and feel my own "apartness" as it felt then. While I was infected with the notion that I was bad, I was nevertheless chronically indignant at the very idea, and constantly seeking to prove to myself that it wasn't true. This led to some pretty convoluted behavior. Defensive, aggressive, and placatory in turn.

I also had a great need to do good and *be* good, to convince myself I was really a good person, not a bad one, and sometimes doing bizarre things to prove it. For example, by going through childbirth without painkilling drugs because they might harm the baby, I proved to myself that I was capable of loving after all. I also needed to get close to others and their feelings, to make me feel less isolated. (Something to make one reflect on people's motivation in helping others!) It was also an energy-consuming way to live, deflecting me from much more normal youthful pursuits.

Seen from either a traditional religious or a psychoanalytic perspective, it was as if our inherited human sinfulness or selfish motivations were confirmed by Hitler's actions, which were reinforced by my later upbringing, and had now to be desperately disproved.

This reminds me that I mustn't generalize. I happened to have two things to deal with: the losses, but also being made to feel a bad person as well. Each person's experience must therefore be different. I had two things to grapple with, which were intertwined. Others had a different mixture of problems.

It's interesting to speculate on the motivations of those who took us in. There were some cases of altruism, and I believe Doris was motivated at first by a liking for my mother and a wish to help. I don't blame her for being unable to sustain it. I don't know if I could even have tried.

Others had other motives. Many of the families were religious, and some were doing their good deed. I remember Doris talking about me in whispers at church, where she was admired for having taken me in. Behind her hand, she would say, "We don't know where her parents are." Many of us hated being the objects of this. We may sound ungracious, but being someone's good deed isn't the basis for childhood happiness because the child is secondary to the needs of the host.

This was often the case. Some hosts were emotionally disturbed, and many children suffered at their hands. Some hosts took in refugees because we came from middle-class homes, which was thought preferable to being forced to accept evacuees from London after its expected bombing, since those people would come from poor homes, in London's East End perhaps, and cause all sorts of trouble. Some took girls of thirteen, fourteen, and fifteen and used them as servants right away. But some did provide secure loving homes. Interestingly, I have not met many of these. Where are they? Maybe they don't need to get together with other refugees because they feel truly integrated. But even they had losses for which they needed to grieve, and I wonder how much even those in happy homes felt it right to grieve for others?

Those I know who have little or no contact with other refugees and seldom or never talk about their experiences somehow strike me as a little bit flat on one side, as if they haven't quite rounded out because they haven't allowed the whole of their feelings to be acknowledged and expressed. And with that, they probably haven't done the grieving that is appropriate. It sounds contradictory, but in some ways grieving is enriching, because you allow yourself depths of feeling that are rich, even if unhappy.

Appropriate unhappiness is a healthy feeling; depression is not. In retrospect I can feel the big difference. In pure grief, we are at one with all humans who suffer and are therefore in a position to share it and be equal with and closer to others. We are not living at a superficial level, pretending that the unhappy things underneath are not there. We don't need to feel inferior anymore when we allow ourselves to grieve. For one thing, this shows courage. I think it enriches us, and if we use it well, it can also enrich our relationships. So grieving in itself is part of the recovery process. This is now so well known that it hardly needs saying, yet when we were young, the whole world around us seemed unaware of it.

At that time, I felt weakened by the losses and my subsequent upbringing, fearing that I would be alone always, and forever vulnerable both to more losses and to other misfortunes. I think this was by far the biggest fear. That the aloneness would go on forever, getting worse the longer it lasted. Some refugees in this position made early marriages, and had any man been foolish enough, I might have done the same. Yet I was also super-cautious. I never forgot that my mother had saved me, and it behooved me to make the very best of my life. This did not feel like a heavy obligation; I think that urge might have been inside me if I'd led a normal life. It also works to my benefit now. When I enjoy myself, I feel it is almost a gift to my mother, what she would have wanted for me all along.

Then I felt compelled to make enormous efforts to become strong, to arm myself against further blows. It never really ends, but with hard work and a long period of good relationships, one can succeed. But I must admit that I think one does need many years of good life experiences to compensate for all that had happened, as well as the psychological help I had, to improve my confidence gradually. I'm afraid hard work alone is not enough. Luck helps, too, and there are some sorrows that need actual life-changing events to heal them. If you are really lucky you can come out strengthened, but it all made for a hard-working, slightly distorted life.

Along with my intense fear of never having a family again, I had a huge fear of losing my first baby; this would be the very first flesh and blood after all the losses. The first true physical belonging. The joke about Jewish mothers being overprotective is not funny. How could we bear more losses? I know that when many of us had babies, we consciously felt we were having replacement children to overthrow Hitler's efforts to obliterate us. It was particularly painful to produce children and feel that there was no one to care except the child's father. Having children is in itself almost a gift to the past generation, the gift of immortality. But there was no past generation to enjoy it. Imagine these minute yet huge repercussions, all because of Hitler, repeated in one way or another inside millions of people.

I had a tremendous craving for "normality." This to me meant being ordinary, having an actual, real family and a "place" where I belonged without question. A casualness and taking for granted in relationships utterly lacking in my experience. I'm sure I had a rosy view of family life at one time, imagining that one needed only to have parents for everything to be all right. To see others lead what looked like normal lives was really hard. They were so relaxed, so apparently complacent. They had a cushion of care under them. Their welfare was of intimate and intense concern to their parents.

I remember once I went on holiday to the Austrian Alps with Anne, an old school friend, and there was an avalanche close by. Of course her parents were on the phone at once. No one even noticed or knew where I was. That was my normality. I lived with this difference every day. My friends, and I did have great ease in making them, would return with baskets of presents after celebrating birthdays with their families. They had somewhere to go for Christmas where they belonged. Normality. It was their ability to take all this for granted that I missed all the time. It sounds pathetic, and I still hate that. I know I expected too much from some friends; they could not provide what I needed, which was a real family.

When I was a child in England, I looked forward to birthdays with painful intensity, counting off the long days on my calendar and then hating the birthday itself. Doris did make an effort. She'd provide a cake, candles, presents. I'd even be allowed to invite up to three children to tea. But it felt all wrong, somehow embarrassing. My mother wasn't there, and it had no meaning for anyone. The whole point of a birthday is not only that the child celebrates the anniversary of his birth but that the mother also celebrates having given birth. It's of profound significance for both. To this day, I feel uncomfortable on my birthday. I want to celebrate, but I'm always glad when it's over.

Of course now I know that my friends' lives, too, were far more complex and difficult than I thought. It was strange that I harbored these illusions, but that was no doubt part of the arrested childish attitudes

I mentioned before. And because I felt so different and deprived, I deluded myself for a long time that their lives were easier and simpler than mine. Eventually, a great many years later, I came to learn that people whose own mothers had mistreated them suffered far worse than I did. I at least had never experienced basic deprivation.

I wanted to work in medicine and psychiatry. I was fascinated by people's feelings from a very young age. My schoolteachers looked sad. I wondered if they had lost men in this war or the last. Yet I still deluded myself that I was alone in my troubles.

It was not until very many years later that I realized my aloneness also gave me the bonus of a kind of freedom. I had no expectations to meet (except the expectation of failure, which I intended not to fulfill) and few family duties or obligations. Hardly anyone to please or placate except, later, my marriage family. I probably didn't realize it early enough to make use of this freedom, and since I lacked the confidence to use it, I would not have done so. I feared risk taking because I didn't want to spoil the life my mother had worked so hard to give me. In any case, I don't know how many people actually like or can use this kind of freedom, in which there is absolutely no emotional web of support to float one along.

I felt I was living several lies. My lively exterior covered chronic sadness and conflict. I didn't admit my Jewishness or foreignness to any new acquaintance, and many of my friends didn't know about it till years later, all because I feared being thought of as dirty and somehow bad, being "different" or pitied, or even just being talked about, as I'd experienced already. In the town where I was brought up, my foster family was what is known as "prominent in the community," and I learned early to be discreet. So I was shielding not only my past but my present. I could not let anyone know what a strange and unhappy home it was.

And though I often say that I don't and didn't expect anti-Semitism to actually kill me in my new land, it's occurred to me lately to wonder if at a deeper level I really did and do. Why else have I continued not to complete forms honestly when asked my ethnic origin? Why else, ultimately, do I keep so silent? Even to this day, after the world has seen so many calamities, the sense of differentness lingers. But, really, we should be taking our experiences in stride by now. And we must take care not to feed on the drama indefinitely.

I've finally come round to notice that I've left out the most important thing in this discussion about being left alone in the world. And that's love. I see why I've left it out; it was absent and became like a foreign land, something quite unfamiliar. It's hard to talk about because its absence was so painful. We actually didn't have any love, most of us, after leaving our parents at such a tender age, until and unless we found partners. We lived for many years without it. Not only the feeling of love, but no hugs or kisses.

My adoptive brother Harry asked me recently if I was ever shown any physical affection by his parents. He said they hadn't shown him any, and I said, no, that I was untouched by human hand. At least I was not abused by human hand either. The worst chastisement I got was a smacking, in cold blood, the day following the sin of reading in bed after my bedtime, which was six o'clock on the dot, even in summer, until I was about thirteen. It took some years to feel I was touchable, deserving of love. My environment had made me feel I was not.

Nowadays, I realize, I'm old enough for most of my friends to be orphans, too, and this shared bereavement, sad to say, adds to the feeling of belonging today. But luckily for me, it is only one among a great many other, happier things I share.

6

Heda, Elsie, Doris, and Me

Heda was my mother's best friend since schooldays, I believe. They ran a Girl Guide troop together, and knew each other well. Heda survived the war by going into hiding, as she describes, instead of assembling for deportation when the order came from the Nazis.

I wrote to her quite a long time after the war, some time in the fifties, to ask her questions about my mother. Unfortunately, her first letter is undated, but the second was written in 1961, and there probably wasn't more than a year or two between them.

Her assumption that I didn't clearly remember my mother is false. On the contrary, I remember her extremely clearly, but I always like to hear other people's views. As adult contemporaries, they would naturally have another perspective.

Karlikova 27,
Praha 6
Stresovice[1]
Dear Milena,

I thought at first that it would be very easy to give a picture of Anka so that her daughter might know what she was like. But when I come to put it down I feel that it is a rather difficult task, to make anyone see Anka as I saw her. We were great friends. But to know someone intimately and to give his features so as to present his personality in full to someone who hardly remembers him, that's quite different.

Heda Kaufmanová, before 1939.

One may well say that Anka was able. Lots of people are. Originally, she herself did not even mean to be able in the sense this word was understood in the family i.e., she did not want to turn to business and be able in business. When we were both girls, she meant to study astronomy. Of course you have to be able for that as well, but the family had no understanding for that sort of ableness. Anka was taken from Secondary school at fifteen and learned shorthand and bookkeeping. When, after some years, she was sitting at her father's dim office in a dim street, which would do credit to any novel by Charles Dickens, she let her steam off by writing little verses, in the way of nursery rhymes:

Here I am, sitting at the table,
like an Abbess very able.

The Abbess being there merely for the sake of the rhyme in the Czech text. In spite of that, she was so able in business that at the age when other girls think of getting married, she went to England as representative of a big house dealing in ready made dresses; she did not fail to make quite big business, just like an old experienced agent.

But this was not why I would call Anka able. Her ableness was in her endeavour to master any situation in life; to learn and to get experience; to handle an axe as well as a needle, just as well as to handle people. As to handling people she was not to be surpassed. A small example; we were a party of five. Anka, her sister Mila, then Milena who was my assistant in the Guide company along with Anka, then Milka with the beautiful voice, and I. Milka's father, an architect, owned some tennis courts he had built. Now Anka, at the age of twenty, had the idea of forming a queer enterprising company out of us five, the 'Tennis Five' and to hire one of these courts. It was an expensive affair. But at the end of the tennis season, Anka, the manager, could pay the expenses and put aside a respectable sum which never was surpassed by any of us alternating in the function of manager. We simply were not able, not in business.

Anyway, the Tennis Five earned enough to enable its members to make a fine trip to Switzerland in 1927. Each of us could spend as much as five Swiss francs a day; this is not much for Switzerland of course, but we slept in student's hostels and fed on Swiss cheese, and fruit, and had a wonderful time wandering from Zurich to Geneva mostly on foot. There still were some francs left to see a bit of France and Italy. It was Anka again who was the instigating element of the enterprise. She outlined the itinerary. Curiously enough, we invariably missed all trains we had to board under her leadership. And yet she led us safely through Furka, Grimsel, Gemipass, down to Geneva and then to Avignon, Arles, Nîmes, Marseilles, Cavalaire, Monaco, Genova, Milano and home again.

Now what is it, to be able, really? To learn languages, to swim, to dance, to be good at skiing and hopeless at tennis, to read and understand verses and music, to be interested in science, history, psychology, to study dietetics and to make all sorts of things with equal interest and zeal, with an almost scientific punctuality and the keen curiosity of an explorer. And to explore above all, human characters. To educate oneself and educate others. Anka was quite wonderful in mastering the art of leading others. She even educated the company council. None but Anka could submit to such minute criticism, and tear to pieces, all my activity as company captain. I felt very small when, friend or no friend, she started her matter of fact remarks in the company council. Of course it was very useful to me and in fact, it was from Anka that I have learned not to fear people, not to fear action, not to fear negotiating with people for the sake of any good purpose. Though, up to now, I hate negotiating with people.

When Anka married Emil, the gay, upright, honest and uncomplicated Emil, one would say, seeing her, that she was running her job of being married and educating her daughter with the same scientific thoroughness and energy she put into any activity of hers. Curious thing now; in spite of all pedagogic theory she had studied, and practiced successfully in the guide's company, she was spoiling you, my dear. Are you still a spoiled child? I do not think so, but you were, at the time we have known each other. I dislike spoiled children and you must have instinctively felt it, because you quite distinctly did not like me, to Anka's apparent regret. Never mind that, I am sure we would get along all right now.

When the Nazis came, you were sent to England. You know all about it, don't you. It was not easy for your parents to decide. But they did wisely, sending you abroad. Otherwise you would have perished with them.

It is hardly possible to make anyone, who did not experience it himself, to see the atmosphere we were living in during war under occupation. There are documents and fiction based on real experience, handling the subject from different aspects. I have no idea how much [of] this material was printed in English. And films have been made, I am sure. But only a very great master of prose, such as Zweig, for instance, could make something out of all the fantastically dreadful material so as to make people see how it really was. We ordinary people can just pick out some facts.

Let's try to pick out some, relative to Anka and her splendid behaviour, her keeping her head, her spirit of cooperation; her doing what she thought was right, and doing it in spite of all danger. Your Grandfather, Anka's father, was imprisoned by the Nazis as early as on October 28th 1939, during the student's demonstrations. He was walking down the street, and some S.S. man did not like your grandfather's nose so he arrested him. He was kept in the Gestapo prison at Charles Place and later on taken to the concentration camp of Oranienburg. After some time the Germans played a nasty comedy with the family, pretending that they would let your Grandpa go, on condition that he receives a visa for some very distant part of the world and leaves the country the very day he arrives from Oranienburg. Anka left no stone unturned. With the help of the Worker's Union she achieved the miracle of getting a visa, for Tenerife if I am not mistaken, and packed her father's belongings so that he might just change the trains in Prague. At that time we had no experience, none of us, with the whole system of perfidity and playing cat and mouse. The very day your Grandpa ought to come from Oranienburg, the family received a note from the Gestapo in Prague saying that he died in Oranienburg 'following to an intestinal infection'.

Later on, Anka and Emil, Mila and her husband, had to leave their flat and remove to the town district designed for Jewish families. This was Prague 1, which used to be the Jewish Ghetto under the Hapsburg regime. It was not now a ghetto exactly, as in Warsaw or later on in Terezin. But the families had to live propped up in old flats—while the modern and good ones were taken by the Germans. There were flats consisting of three rooms, for instance, occupied by fourteen people, and the kitchen and accessories serving to all. Anka and Emil had quite a nice room to themselves in such a flat. Emil was working with the Jewish Community and Anka was busy working with Jewish children. All those who had joined the Jewish community had a chance of not being sent to Terezin or some Polish concentration camp too early.

Later on I had common work with Anka; we were smuggling food to prisoners in the Gestapo prison at Charles Place, where my brother was imprisoned since October 1941. He found ways and means how to distribute the food received, among his comrades.

But most of Anka's time and energy was devoted to children. You were safe in England. So Anka thought it was her turn to do something for children who lacked proper care. You must know that the Nazis did not allow Jewish children in occupied territories to go to school. Children of all ages, wearing the yellow star with JUDE printed in black on it, were loitering in streets while other Czech children were at school. The phenomenon was too conspicuous, even the Nazis had to see it. So they allowed the children to gather in some rooms in order 'to be kept busy' as the term was, and this institution was given the proud name of 'Children's Homes'. Of one of this 'Home' Anka became responsible. With an experienced teacher, Jirina Picková, later on executed at Osvecim [Auschwitz] she devised a plan how to educate and teach children who have not been allowed to learn.

No books, no notebooks. Also no exams. Just the knowing 'how' from the part of the two people in charge and their never tiring will to achieve as much as possible in the way of schooling and education under the very nose of the Gestapo. The keen and eager children learned by playing, singing, reciting, simply anything that could pass under the label of being kept busy. Anka ran a double risk; the Gestapo could find out, after all, that the children were getting as a well-rounded education as the situation would allow. Second, the children got an idea of the Czech culture and tradition. Most probably no one will ever give due publicity and credit to that patient and dangerous work of Anka. One may as well shrug one's shoulders and say that it was no use anyhow, seeing that most of those children went East to concentration camps and gas rooms. Well, I don't know; was it no use to give children moments of joy they were entitled to, and handle them as normally as possible in times fantastically abnormal, crazy, 'out of joint'? Moreover, was it no use that Anka had chosen little Ralph from the Jewish Orphanage and tried to make a human being out of a creature neglected and animal like? Of course, finally, little Ralph had to go East and perished with hundreds or thousands of other children in some distant concentration camp. But he had known happy days with Anka and Emil, he had known the flavour of home. Was it no use?

When I got on the transport list for Terezin Anka came and said, Don't go, dive. If you still have the sparkle of the possibility you had before your brother's arrestation, don't go, dive. I have had news that the transports to Terezin are but an interlude to total annihilation. Dive. Well, I did.

After some time the Gestapo was after me, they found out that I was keeping up the connection with my imprisoned brother and his comrades. They were also after my sister in law; she had a nervous breakdown in her hiding spot, but Anka took her to the 'home' she was in charge of and gave her shelter for one night there, before Irma could be put safe again.

Just think of it; giving a night's accommodation to a person looked for by the Gestapo, now, was Anka able? She herself and Emil could have found a hiding spot when due to the transport; we have been spinning out schemes again and again. Unfortunately, their appearance, conspicuously Jewish at first sight, was a heavy handicap, almost insurmountable. Same as in the case of Mila's son Paul who, but for his typically Jewish physiognomy, could have been sheltered in a Czech children's Home. In summer 1943 Anka and Emil went to Terezin and then to Auschwitz in Poland. Our old friend Ela, who met Anka in Auschwitz, said to me after the war that Anka continued working with children in Auschwitz. There were lots of grown ups who, among the constant terror, misery and death could not 'keep on keeping on'. They perished simply because their mind and spirit was not strong enough, always provided they were not murdered right away.

So one cannot but admire the spirit of Anka who amidst of all the daily misery could still find time and energy to work with children just as she tried to work with them in Prague. Ela says also that Anka had good warm clothing and shoes. He who has read Norbert Fryd's novel 'Krabice Zivych', 'The Box of the Living' can have an idea about what it meant to have shoes, and keep having them, in a concentration camp. Shoes meant life.

Was Anka able? and yet she did not survive, because the brutal force smashed her. One day, it was on March 7th, Ela told me, in 1944 if I am not mistaken, the whole transport with which she came from Terezin to Osvecim, was taken to the gas-room. They knew where they were going to. While they marched in, they were all singing Kde Domov Muj,—'Where is my home'—the Czech National Anthem, so Ela says.

You might feel there was already too much of this war stuff. Yet it had to be said, at least the main things I can remember. Of course, going back in my mind, I can still find lots of moments, merry and full of real happiness we both had spent before the war. I still can visualise Anka climbing our northern border mountains, always two steps behind me, and loitering among blackberries, which she simply had to eat up, all of them, heedless of the miles we still had ahead. I can see her, sitting on her trunk full packed, on our way to England in 1929, and trying hard to shut it, and the trunk bursting open again and again, and when she succeeded in shutting it, she had to open it again because of some important object to be fished out of the hopeless chaos inside. How queer; Anka the systematic person, the organisational genius, never could find her toothbrush which, after an hour's investigation appeared to have got quite mysteriously into one of her shoes.

She went to England armed with a huge notebook and spent her time collecting idioms and slang. She noted carefully whether the slang in question was a bad one; in that case she put a little star behind it in her notebook. There was slang with two stars, too, and behold, with three stars. When we were invited to tea with some friends, Anka started, quite unexpectedly, reciting her slangs, the star spangled as well, to the great amusement of our English friends. They finished to acquire Anka's way of speaking English; they kept saying, 'oh, you know, it's just a little something else' and other Ankaisms. And they never tired of teaching Anka slang, bad slang and very bad slang. Is it shocking? We were terribly glad they did not find things shocking, and that they were just as merry and free and full of beans as we both were at that time.

I am afraid I did not say half of what I should have said of Anka. Was she with faults? Certainly, just as all of us. But she was good as bread is good, and a rare specimen of harmony between brain and heart. If Anka were alive, my own life after the war would be a hundred times easier. And this is the best you can learn about Anka.

Heda

Sresovice Hospital,

Praha November 1960

1. There were two addresses, one at the beginning and another at the end of this letter. I know that Heda spent the postwar years in and out of hospitals, usually with bronchial problems.

Heda's health was extremely poor after her years in hiding, and she suffered badly from chest infections and asthma. On one occasion I was able to send her some penicillin from England; Czechoslovakia was then in the grip of the Communists, and I believe she had difficulty in getting the drugs and antibiotics she needed. That may have been normal under the Communists. I also had the impression that she suffered from depression and loneliness. She, too, had lost most of her family, and in particular her beloved brother. I don't know whether she ever had the opportunity to marry, or if she wanted to. I think she forgave my having been a spoiled child, for when acknowledging the penicillin, she commented in the third, lost, letter that it was exactly what my mother would have done—her highest praise!

Her life sounded bleak indeed, as were, and even now are, the lives of many survivors of the Nazis. The Czechs in fact had barely time to catch their breath before the Communists took over and began another reign of terror. I learned only in later years that those people, both children and adults, in every country in Europe, who went into hiding suffered a peculiarly isolated form of misery, in most cases far worse than ours. Unlike us, they were on enemy-occupied soil and were in daily danger of being discovered and murdered. They were hidden in convents or children's homes, or with Catholic and Protestant families in the countryside. Many adults and even children on their own had to dash and creep from one refuge to another, which might be a farmhouse or barn, pigsty or shed, and even caves or sewers, never knowing how close their pursuers were or whether the people who saw them were friendly or would report them to the Gestapo. They didn't even know if they'd be able to forage anything to eat. Many had to hide in partitioned cellars, attics, and closets. They saw others threatened with death or actually killed; they knew that their protectors risked death by hiding them. Many lost the rest of their families as well, or didn't know their fate at all. They certainly had no definable group of peers at war's end. Until recently, they were not acknowledged either individually or as a group that had suffered terribly. I myself did not know what a large number existed.

I had heard already what a poor welcome many camp survivors received when they tried to return to their hometowns and start life again. Now we know that the hidden people had equal difficulties. It was not until 1991 that the first gathering of formerly hidden children took place in New York, and articles in the general press told the world about them. And now, with memoirs and accounts published, they have their own associations and means of getting help and are also a focus of interest to scholars and many others. Heda did not live to see this.

Among another pile of correspondence that Doris gave me I found many letters addressed to her from the Guiding friends in the Midlands. They not only described all the efforts they, too, were making to get us all out (and this is how some of the duplications, muddles, and eventual acrimony arose) but provided nuggets of information I hadn't known before. For instance, the women tried very hard to get Heda, her brother the doctor, and her mother to jobs and safety. One of them, Elsie, with whom Doris locked horns repeatedly, described Heda when recommending her for a hospital job:

> I suppose it must be someone with experience for Salisbury? They wouldn't take Heda? She has no medical qualifications, but is a sound, calm, reliable person and would be very soothing I should think. Or could they take a man, Viktor Kaufmann, her brother, also a doctor? Heda is 34, so is too old perhaps to train as a probationer? She is such a nice girl, a very lovely character, but not quite so vivacious and taking [appealing] as Anka. I don't think you met her? She was Overseas Secretary for Czechoslovakia. However, I expect she will have to have a domestic job. She could be a nursery governess though, if that is allowed, or a companion to an old lady.

Elsie also related in a letter dated April 6, 1939, that one of her friends was in Vienna when the Germans marched in and saw them make Jewesses scrub the streets with a mixture of water and chemicals so strong that the skin came off their hands, which started bleeding. So we can see that efforts to help started quite quickly after the German invasion of Czechoslovakia on March 15.

In another letter, dated March 22, she deplored the fact that the Czech friends would have to take menial jobs and added: "If they can only reach safety before any of them are thrown into concentration camps."

So some knowledge of the camps did exist among the general public in England by this time, although I don't know from what date. But Elsie quoted Heda as having given her this information, so perhaps it was known chiefly by people who had contacts in Europe. Another Girl

Guide friend, Sally, wrote to Doris about my missing guarantee* and remarked:

> I do so wish we had them all here. Anka now weighs six stone [84 pounds] less than she has ever done since she's been an adult. Poor girl, she must be worried to death. She is also attending cookery classes, in spite of being a good cook. I sampled her meals in 1936.

It is also clear from Elsie's letters that she, too, had all the information necessary for bringing refugees over. Like my mother, she wrote pages about permits, guarantors, the need for jobs, the difficulty of placing the men, and the urgency, since some men seemed to be arrested before their families were deported.

Most of the major towns in England had refugee committees, and the central one was at Bloomsbury House, in London. It is from there that Nicholas Winton, whose part in saving us we learned about later, did some of his work, helped by his mother. I have a letter concerning my permit, signed by him, with the heading "British Committee for Refugees

* The British government, while giving way to pressure to allow 10,000 refugee children into Britain, was anxious to ensure that they never became a charge on the State and therefore required every prospective host family to fulfill certain safeguards. The family had to pay 50 pounds Sterling per child. This was to cover the cost of the journey to England, plus a further journey on to another country: in theory, the children were supposed to be in transit to other destinations. Since the average wage in Britain was at that time 500 pounds per year, rescuing a child required dedication and financial means on the host's part. The host family also had to sign a guarantee, undertaking to support the child until the age of eighteen. My guarantee, which Arthur Campbell had signed, was somehow mislaid, and thus Elsie took the trouble to travel to London to try to help find it. She described the visit she made to this office at that very time: "While I was in that room I saw forms ranged in order all over tables, with photos attached, some of beautiful children; you've no idea of the shock it gives one to think of all these little people having to leave their parents." I don't know if I would have made it to Britain without the guarantee; the urgency was so great that some children were admitted without one and were placed in hostels until guarantees could somehow be found for them. Our own parents had to provide health certificates, birth certificates, and various other proofs of identity and status before the precious permit, of which my mother writes so constantly, could be issued by the refugee committee working under such pressure in Prague. Only when both forms—permit and guarantee—had been obtained could a place on a train be reserved.

from Czechoslovakia, Children's Section." The guarantee for me had been lost, and he asked that another one be forwarded immediately.

Nicholas Winton and his mother found foster homes for many of these children, who did not have privately arranged homes to go to as I did, by advertising in newspapers. I was unaware of any of this until about twelve years ago.

Altogether, there were many people and agencies working on our behalf, but it was all immensely hurried. Mostly only those involved knew about it, and I myself am getting a clearer picture only now.

Elsie frequently mentioned that there were six of them working on the problem in her own town, all Guiders. They obviously attacked this rescue operation with Guiding zeal! But none of them was financially well off, and she had to think long and hard before committing herself to supplying guarantees. Both the financial and the moral responsibility weighed on her. But once she decided, she said she made her offer "wholeheartedly."

At the same time, my Czech uncle in London was also joining in attempts to get visas and permits. This could not have been easy for him as he, too, was a refugee, was new to the country's systems, and his English was not yet perfect.

Elsie revealed something else I didn't know: that my father's agreement to let me go alone was quite hard won on my mother's part. It was not until June 26, 1939, that Elsie received a letter from my mother, saying that Emil had finally agreed. This was less than a month before I actually traveled, and only two months and a bit before war broke out.

Heda wrote me at least three letters in the fifties and sixties, but the following is unfortunately the only other one I kept. I don't know if it was chance or the internal conflict her letters evoked that caused me to lose the third one. I wanted to hear about my parents, but Heda's ambivalence, depression, and suffering anger, with its painful reminder of the warring cultures inside me, made her letters difficult reading. I remember one slightly patronizing and threatening sentence: "You would not have survived, my dear, the system crushed everyone." Her letters also made me think of the terrified old relations I'd left behind and the fate I'd escaped myself.

Karliková 27,
Praha 6
Stresovice
December 13th 1961
Dear Milena,

I am very sorry to have been so very long in answering your letter. I was so pleased at receiving it that I wanted to write on the spur of the moment. Unfortunately, as it invariably happens with me, there were heaps of other things to be done before. Thus I went on postponing my answer and here I am at last writing to you after nearly a year. Oh, gosh, life IS a mess. One of my friends who came to see me last week for half an hour or so, cannot imagine how a retired person can have hectic times.

'What are you doing all the day long?' she asked me. The usual lack of imagination even with people trained in a medical line, for they have never experienced in their own skin what it means to be short of breath or even have asthmatic attacks and try to get through the daily routine of washing, tidying up, getting one's meals somehow, without any help, having to ask good neighbours, who are busy from morning till night, to help with the coal, with shopping, etc, and having to solve other sick people's problems.

Now enough of it. For the delay in my correspondence, a few bronchitises and 'flus also are responsible, along with a sudden change in my quarters. I moved to this part of town in May.

I don't know if I'll be able to give you satisfactory information about what your father was like. I have not seen much of him really. I liked him. Can't say he was what one generally calls a good-looking man. But I liked him more than all those splendid looking chaps who courted Anka ever since her first dancing lesson. Emil was honest and sincere and a good sport as far as I could see. He was not tall, on the contrary; very slender, had quick, vivid gestures, there was a sort of elasticity in his movements. He must have been good at gymnastics as a boy. His smile was very broad, and contrasted with a very grave face he put on when telling a joke. Had lots of hobbies, music, languages, gardening, chicken breeding, aquarium and what not. And skillful in all odd jobs he was. His chief interest in music was opera and he had a very good collection of discs, all sorts of quite famous names including Caruso. His mother tongue seemed to be French as well as Italian; he was not born in our country. He spoke Czech very fluently but with a distinct French accent. He had met Anka in one of these clubs called Cercle Français, or Circolo Italiano that were swarming with people wanting to keep up or brush up their foreign languages. I think he fell in love with your Ma at first sight. Well, that's about all I can remember today.

Of your grandparents I am going to tell you another time. Let's hope I won't be so long in writing to you again, as I was this time.

You will most probably hear something more about your mother from another good friend. Her name is also Milena, and she is living in London and was asking for your address in her recent letter to me. She said she'd like to see you and tell you how splendid your mother was. If I am not mistaken you have seen her once at Zdena's. Milena is one of the most clever and fine sort I ever met in my life. I am sure you'll like her, far more than Elsie. By the way, could you not drop a line or two to Elsie? I am sure she'd be glad to have some news from you. I am afraid, she feels rather lonely. Do not forget that it was she who finally persuaded your parents to send you abroad after the Nazi invasion. And she was pulling strings and moving mountains to get your parents abroad too. It is not her fault that she did not succeed in that.

Now, be well, sweet maid and write again. Of course you go on calling me Heda—what else? I would be cross with you if you would not. What about your tonsils? And tell me about your work, please, I am very interested. And have you a spare photograph of yours? You can make me a nice Christmas present by sending me one.

love to you and best Christmas wishes,

Heda

Stresovice Hospital,

Prague

November 1960[1]

1. Again, the address and date at the beginning and end of her letter don't match, indicative, no doubt, of the hard life she was leading and her frequent stays in hospital.

And this, I believe, is the last I heard from her. Alas, I don't think she did write to me about my grandparents. She was yet another casualty of the Nazis, even though she lived through the war.

Only today, while writing this, did I think to phone Aunt Zdena and ask what had happened to Heda. She said that non-Jewish friends in a suburb of Prague hid Heda during the war in some corner of their apartment for three years. She had to be silent, in case neighbors heard and gave them all away. After the war, she was able to work for only a few years because of her asthma and retired early on a pension. Her brother was executed for being in the Resistance. One day in the seventies, a family friend tried to make arrangements to call on Heda a few weeks in advance of a planned visit to Prague, only to be told by Heda that she "would not be available." When some other friends, in whose apartment she lived at that time, returned from a holiday, they found Heda dead. She had killed herself.

She, too, as is shown in the letters from Elsie, knew the Guiding friends in England, all of whom were following the war in Europe closely and with great anxiety as to the fate of their Czech friends.

This letter was written fifteen days after V-E (Victory in Europe) Day by Elsie, the woman with whom Doris had the most disputes regarding my schooling, upbringing, behavior, and, ultimately, home.

May 23rd 1945

Dear Mrs Campbell,

This morning I received a letter from Heda in Prague, sent on from Wales by a returning prisoner of war. Heda has been hidden by friends for three years, and for two years has not been out of doors. She is very exhausted, and now in bed with bronchitis after her first walk in freedom. Her brother who was a doctor was captured in 1941 and sentenced to death in 1945. Her mother was sent to Poland but her sister in law escaped the same way as Heda. I don't know whether you will wish to tell Milena what comes next until we hear more definite news.

Anka was sent to Terezin and then to Poland (Auschwitz) in July 1943. Perhaps she escaped the worst by some miracle. We must just go on hoping.

Heda says very few old people or children are likely to return from concentration camps. They were killed by the thousand in gas-filled rooms.

When I think of Heda's mother, a gentle courteous old lady who wouldn't harm anyone, it makes my blood boil. She doesn't mention Emil. I wonder how long it will be before proper communication is restored.

Heda has asked me to pass on the news of her safety to her other friends here so I must get on with it. My love to Milena. I hope that she will be able to visit me soon, now that travelling is safer. At present I am trying to fix up a holiday with Mother, since I think she will be well enough to travel this summer and she needs a holiday very much. So do I. When the dates of this are fixed I will let you know, and then we can fix up for Milena to come here for a few weeks. She must be loyal to her Mother and Father's wishes.

If you hear anything from Prague, will you please let me know immediately, and I, of course, will send any news I may receive to you.

Heda was Overseas Secretary for all Czechoslovakia, so she may hear something soon through her old Guide friends. I hope she gets back her old post in the Institute of Public Health.

Yours sincerely,
Elsie

To Doris, this letter would have been a red rag to a bull. She had long since cast aside this well-meaning friend as an interfering bossy fool and a competitor for control of my upbringing. It is a mystery why Doris wanted to retain responsibility for me. I never did visit Elsie again. In fact, I think I simply could not have spread my loyalties any wider, and I am afraid I allowed myself to share Doris's prejudice against her for some time. Judging from the conflicting complaints they voiced about each other and me, I must have been utterly confused and chose the easy option of siding with the aggressor.

Doris kept copies of her replies to Elsie, so I have the whole quite extensive conflict before me, sixty years later. The argument seemed extraordinarily important to both of them. Elsie's letters were outspoken, Doris's offensive.

Their ways of life and expectations of me were totally different. Elsie, being a teacher, had big plans for my education and wrote: "Is Milena getting Physics, Chemistry, Biology, Latin and Music?" She continued over a long period to lecture Doris about the small and, in her opinion, useless private schools I was being sent to.

But she was also sexually inexperienced and expressed shock at my normal curiosity about boys:

> Please don't think of me as a bespectacled squeamish spinster. Having slept next door to a medical student friend for four years, who parked her private skeleton under her bed and brought bits of it on to the lawn frequently, there is little I don't know about anatomytis.

I seem to have been sent back and forth between both homes, causing astonishment at my inconsistent behavior.

My aunt Zdena had the labor of ferrying me about England whenever one of these moves took place. She even tried to act as peacemaker, apologizing for the trouble I was causing and trying to placate both women. She wrote to Doris:

> I know that it is not an easy task to have Milena. The house must always be full of her. She is so temperamentful. But she is very clever and very obedient too, isn't she. I think she is so excitable because she had so many experiences, many more than other children her age. And I think her brain is sometimes too quick for her age, what do you think? I am glad and grateful you have seen to her Czech reading, I thought it was the reason she did not forget.

My aunt continued with reiterations of gratitude for Doris's care of me and assurances that she knows Doris must be very kind, as I love her so much. There is talk of my nervous twitching and blinking, and Aunt Zdena comments that she is sure this will be cured by glasses. She also tries to explain how sincere and well-meaning Elsie really is.

Elsie was shocked because I made disparaging remarks about Czechoslovakia and my mother. She wrote in March 1940:

> I find it a little distressing that she has forgotten all her old admiration for her mother. There seems to be an inferiority complex where anything Czech is concerned. I wonder if the children at school have ridiculed her or what is at the bottom of it. [It was not the school!]

Each claimed that I cried bitterly when faced with the prospect of visiting (or leaving!) the other. In fact, I do remember being unable to cope with any further moves, however short, without tears, for many years.

In not one among the many letters is there mention of the trauma of leaving my parents and country as explanation for my behavior, nor did anyone express the idea that shuttling a child between strangers after such a loss might have been disturbing. But this was normal for the time. Elsie really was a kind person, and her heart went out to those children in the photos she saw at Bloomsbury House who had to leave their families. The wartime British evacuees, sent from London to escape the bombing, suffered the same insensitivity toward their feelings about being separated from their families. Physical safety was the uppermost and only consideration. Not until John Bowlby wrote in the fifties about the results of separating child and parent did such understanding even begin to seep into general consciousness.

Elsie did not deserve the contempt with which Doris treated her. She was, I'm sure, a lonely person who desperately needed a child to look after. Her insecurities showed in an awkward manner, but she truly needed to love someone. She continued to keep in touch with me for many years, and I can remember feeling irritated by her letters telling me that she—yet another person!—had saved my life. I knew too little then of how hard she'd worked. Now I wish that I'd visited her when I became an adult, but I probably could not cope with her neediness at the time.

On rereading the letters, I see that Doris and Elsie were inadvertently duplicating their efforts to bring us all to safety—I suppose because my mother had asked both her English friends for help—and with women of such determined opinions, clashes and a break in relations were inevitable. Also, there had been a genuine agreement between Doris,

Elsie, and my mother that I should be shared between the two until my mother was settled in a job and could look after me herself. I would go to Elsie to be educated, as she was the schoolteacher, and spend the holidays with Doris. Each woman had signed guarantees, which became confused as the situation changed. Elsie understandably persisted in pressing her claims for me, feeling that she could provide the best education and fulfill her promises to my mother, whereas Doris felt she had the more recent claim, since she had been ready to provide work and a home for all three of us. She did not tolerate interference or criticism, ever, and had to win this battle as she did all others, even though childcare was not her forte.

A final memorable scene took place at our garden gate, a scene that Doris thoroughly enjoyed; she loved a rout. With arm and finger outstretched, she dismissed Elsie and her interfering ways forever. Elsie was indeed quiet until the war ended, and I remained in one place.

And then Aunt Zdena told me her last story about Elsie. It concerned Elsie's visit to London at the time my guarantee was missing, and Elsie herself describes this visit to the Refugee Headquarters at Bloomsbury House, in one of her letters to Doris. She traveled to London from the Midlands by train, bringing her beloved little dog, her substitute child. She stayed with Zdena in her tiny room, and one afternoon went shopping, leaving the dog in my aunt's care. The dog disappeared; Elsie was frantic with grief, and after a desperate search, went home. Two weeks later, the almost hairless, cadaverous, and exhausted dog limped into his home. It had been 150 miles from door to door. . . .

7
Recovery

As recently as 1988, none of the Kindertransport reunions, the recognition, even the currently open discussion of Jews or the Holocaust, had properly happened. The effects of the losses, although so long ago, were still remarkably raw. The world's press did not mention us, and nor did those who knew us mention what had happened. And, to fit in with the general silence, nor did we. Even those of us who had some therapy to help us with the aftereffects, and were leading good lives with families and careers, still felt isolated in the world, with a strange "adrift" feeling, without real family backgrounds and without colleagues who shared the same experiences. I can remember it clearly. I saw myself as being somehow out on the edge of the world.

At that time, I felt that survivors of the camps had been recognized as having suffered the ultimate. But what of us escapers, those whose suffering was seen as so much less, even nonexistent, that it was never even acknowledged? It seemed to me that the effects of the killings must have rippled down through the generations. It's hard to believe now, but just that short time ago, many of us escapers didn't know of each other's existence. We had arrived on the trains, many children together but too young to connect the significance of our shared experience. Even that it *was* shared. We were not quite as alone as we thought. It is a tragedy that we didn't realize it earlier. Our lives might have been a great deal easier. On the other hand, I wonder if we weren't then ready. To resolve all this, you have, as I said before, to take on a complicated persona and accept the mixture that is yourself. We were not English exactly, nor were we entirely Jewish or European. Perhaps we just couldn't encompass the complexity for many years. We certainly needed one another before we could do so.

I felt in 1984 that I must write about it and also try to meet and perhaps interview others with a similar experience. The strange thing is that this had already been done in 1966 by Karen Girshon. I actually read her book, yet somehow it didn't penetrate my sense of isolation. When I look at that book now, I see that it does give rather short and fragmentary anecdotes from a large number of people. But why I didn't feel any connection with them, or find the book helpful, or become fully aware that my experience really wasn't unique, I cannot understand. I think I even forgot the book existed. Not only was a record of our history missing, but all expression of feeling attached to it was thereby wiped out.

This must have been part of the collusive silence. We perpetuated our own sense of isolation. I wonder now whether we had absorbed the destructive influences around us to such an extent that in some unconscious way we felt we had to continue to suffer. Perhaps it had even become a habit. So I sat down and wrote, and my words were much more impassioned than they would be now, because there have been many healing experiences since and I can take a much more detached view.

In 1984, I wrote:

> Much has been written about the Holocaust—the suffering, the killings, the families ruined and scattered. Six million killed. Many with no one left to mourn. There are no words left to express it all. But what of those who "escaped"? I think of that entire period as a giant stone, sunk into the world's pool, its ripples eddying even unto a seventh generation.
>
> It is about the second and third generation that I want to write. Not only must the world never forget the wrong done to those who were killed, but those eddies reaching unto all those generations must be recognised as part of the whole; that the "sin we do unto one we do unto all."
>
> This is the story of one who "escaped." But there is no escape. We in families are one flesh; what is done to one is done to all. Tear us apart, and

a gaping, bleeding wound is left. Kill one member, those remaining are less. This sounds like melodrama. It is, but it's true. Even those of us who endured it sometimes wonder if it really truly happened. We have lived with it for 47 years. So long! Shouldn't you forget it, you say? We wonder what it feels like to be a normal person. I cannot imagine what it is like to grow up in a family whose members die by natural means. Even a divided family, separated by divorce, emigration, death, is still in the normal natural world. There is something wholly unnatural to have belonged to and been torn from a family which was systematically, deliberately, rounded up and killed less humanely than cattle. By the accident of birth, to be marked by one madman as fit only for extermination. While the world watched and colluded. What can that do to the escapers' self-worth? But growing beyond that, to the worth of the human family? The meaning of it all. The meaning of God. No one knows. We grope, all of us, in the dark.

This narrative is the story of just one, who escaped in body, but who, despite the personal efforts to prevail over injury and loss, still lives every day with the emptiness that such nearly total family loss brings. There must be many such others. But we do not have a club. Strangely, though there are survivor associations, meetings, memorials, and now a huge body of Holocaust literature, there is somehow a hush about escapers. Almost as if, with our lesser suffering, we are a lesser breed. This is not paranoia. No one has inflicted this persona on us. We have done it to ourselves. Our sufferings ARE less. That is the trouble. They pale into insignificance when we compare them with the gas chambers, the starvation, the tortures, that we escaped. Perhaps we are even ashamed? Do we feel unworthy of such escape? We think of our parents, our beloved grandparents. Our survival has an enormity, an impertinence, when measured against their unwarranted deaths. When we think of their characters, they take on a nobility which would surely not have been theirs had we experienced the normal struggle for independence that adolescence brings.

Those are the words I wrote then, in rather purple prose unlike my usual self, and yet I must have felt so strongly to have written them. Mercifully, they are out of date now. Today we escapers do now have a club, and we even have a name, Reunion of Kindertransport. We've had our reunions, we know where to contact one another, we've made friends with those of similar experience, and we know how we all feel, but my words are significant in describing the evolution of our joint history. That so much time should have elapsed, and so much suffering been experienced alone, because somehow we and the world couldn't see that we had a right to be recognized! This is another thing that should not be allowed to happen again. But I'm afraid it will. It seems that time must pass before those who suffer and those who should listen are able to get in touch with each other.

Fortunately, we've also recognized that our children and grandchildren have been affected, although until recently they too were ignored; now things have improved for them as well, because of this recognition. Now they too have a club which they can join if they feel the need. The effects on them were varied, too.

As in the case of camp survivors, some of us spoke about our experiences too often, some not enough. In some families, a sort of unspoken pall of past suffering hung over the home. In others, the problems might surface in extreme overprotection, in a general atmosphere of insecurity and paranoia, and in an intolerant attitude toward the perceived minor suffering of others, comparing it always with "You don't know what suffering is." We might create a chronic atmosphere of "outsiderness" or indulge in excessive frugality and even hoarding.

Many of us felt silently guilty about complaining of any pain or problem, tending to use the camp experience of our fantasies as the yardstick to measure it against. But I want to emphasize a distinction between feeling guilty for complaining and feeling guilty for surviving. I certainly do not feel the latter. That would be crazy and wrong; I think the generalized notion of survivor guilt has been grossly overstated. Guilt for the killing lies with the Germans. But unease at complaining of trivialities, yes, I think many of us feel that.

We also had difficulty with the normal disciplining of our children, or with asking for help from them or anyone else, because we retained the feeling of "having no rights." Naturally, our children didn't understand the origins of these behaviors, and the effects could be quite subtle and unspoken, as, for example, in the case of parents who felt so deprived themselves that they were unable to communicate warmth and security to their children. All these things can now be talked about and recognized as a commonly experienced and shared problem among the second and third generations of younger people.

In 1989, five years after I had written the words above, I decided to get in touch with Vera Gissing, a fellow Czech who had organized a fairly recent reunion of former pupils at the Czech school in Wales, where I, too, had spent a term. Before my eleventh birthday, Arthur and Doris realized that I had forgotten every word of my native tongue, and if my parents survived I would be unable to speak to them, so they decided to send me to the Czech school in Wales, which had been set up for expatriate Czech children for just this purpose. It was a thoughtful and well-meaning thing for them to do.

Interestingly enough, in saying that I had never met anyone with my experience, I show how selective one's memory is. Of course I had met these Czech children. I have a diary I wrote at the time that reveals my excitement at the prospect of going to a "boarding school"—made glamorous in my mind by my books of schoolgirl stories. I believe the words "train," "leaving your family," or even "Jew" never entered my head, and in any case I found everything Czech too painful to think about. As far as I was concerned, this just happened to be a school for Czechs.

Yet they were trying to teach us Hebrew, and I still didn't make the connection! I was eleven and must have been denying like crazy. But I have a friend now, Vera Schaufeld, with an experience almost identical to my own, who did exactly the same thing. She, too, was at the Czech school, was being brought up by middle-class Brits in the provinces, and felt as isolated as I did. We didn't know each other at the school.

But maybe as children we were quite unable to deal with the complexities. The school was a disaster from my point of view, and I didn't learn any Czech that anyone could notice. I couldn't adapt to what had become an alien environment again. Czechs seemed foreign now. The children were much more precocious than I was, and I can remember my total confusion. But above all I was wracked with homesickness and lived for letters from Doris! She and Arthur took pity on me at the end of one term and allowed me to return to them.

I was beginning to feel I'd like to meet and interview people with a similar experience and maybe write a book about it. Even at that stage it had not dawned on my mind how necessary this was for my own healing, yet I was inching toward it. After we had met once, Vera Gissing phoned me and said, "Watch the Esther Rantzen show on Sunday night. Also read the *Sunday Mirror.*"

So I did, and for the first time, there on TV, I saw us Train Kids talked about.

We heard for the first time about Nicholas Winton, the leader of the four men and three women who organized the Prague children with travel permits, got them onto trains, and in some cases managed to find foster homes for them. He had apparently found the list of us Czech children in his attic quite recently and wondered what to do with it. He passed it to Elizabeth Maxwell, wife of the newspaper tycoon Robert Maxwell, who was Jewish and had been born in Czechoslovakia, because he knew of her interest in the Holocaust.

She was then, unbeknownst to us, organizing a big Holocaust conference, "Remembering for the Future," at Oxford. We were later invited to the London part of this conference. Thus it got into the *Sunday Mirror* through her husband, who meanwhile passed the information on to Esther Rantzen, who made it a topic of her BBC television show.

That is how it all began. I saw us Train Kids discussed on TV. Hitherto we had been unheard of among the British public, and even among ourselves. Almost every one of us had felt isolated, too young at the time to have grasped that there were 10,000 of us who had been allowed into Britain and must therefore be alive somewhere, perhaps experiencing the same things. This isolation applied particularly to those put into English Christian homes, but even those in Jewish homes or in hostels with other children like themselves still found they were in an alien environment, without any real family and without anyone to share their experiences or offer them any comfort. At the end of the BBC program, the audience watching at home was told, if any of them had been on one of the trains, to get in touch with the BBC. I can still remember how the hairs stood up on the back of my neck when the girl at the BBC, consulting her list, told me that, yes, my name was there. Remember, it hadn't been mentioned for fifty years, since it happened, and suddenly we were public knowledge. Hitherto I hadn't known that there *was* a list.

We were all invited to the BBC to meet Esther Rantzen and Nicholas Winton. Right away some of us made friends and started to meet, spending hours exchanging experiences. Finally, healing had begun in earnest.

This was the beginning, then, after all these years, of recognition and recovery, as we gradually learned the story of our rescue. Some details of the story are only now beginning to emerge with any clarity and still need some piecing together, as most of the participants have died and left either incomplete or no records.

As I've said before, in some ways our disappearance into the background was self-imposed, motivated in many cases by fear of the anti-Semitism ingrained in the British psyche at that time. Although we did not consciously expect to be rounded up and killed, we did fear the rejection and hostility implicit in the attitude that Jews were somehow dirty and inferior, people to be whispered about disparagingly, who partly deserved their fate. I think some of us did not want to be exposed as Jewish, *just in case* another madman should be let loose, and I think we actually *did* fear being "caught next time."

Also, of course, many of us had become Anglicized and were ambivalent about our mixed background for just these reasons; we were rather fiercely identifying with being, or seeming, British. This ploy threw us into the position of living a lie, a very uncomfortable state, which some of us, even now, have not wholly relinquished. Those of us who had arrived in England very young found the temptation to live this lie very great. We were brought up in a wholly British environment, in British families which regarded foreigners and Jews as very foreign indeed, even despicable. What emotional option did we have but to identify with our surroundings and hide our original background? Especially since no one was interested in hearing about it. Also, because of our young age, we lost our original speaking accent, so our apparent Britishness was complete.

The final stage of our exit from Prague seems to have been instigated by Doreen Warriner, a lecturer from the London School of Economics already working in Prague for the British Committee for Refugees. She was chiefly occupied in trying to free refugees from Sudetenland, displaced at the time of Hitler's annexation there, who were still being held in unhappy and unhealthy transit camps, since they had nowhere else to go. Some of these were active political Social Democrats and on the Gestapo's "wanted" list; others had simply fled or been ousted by the invader. These were the people my mother mentions in one of her letters, in December 1938, as having nowhere to go. The route through Poland, which Doreen Warriner was obliged to organize, was not entirely legal from the German point of view, so she was at constant risk herself.

She was thus so busy that she couldn't cope with the Jewish children, who also needed someone to organize their escape. Martin Blake, who came as an emissary from the Refugee Committee in London, became aware of this need and called his old friend Nicholas Winton, with whom he had been about to leave for a skiing holiday, to come and help. Nicholas Winton saw at once that these children with permits to travel and enter England needed someone to pull the threads together and get children, foster homes, and trains coordinated. He became the main organizer, working from both Prague and London, but two other men, Bill Barazetti and Trevor Chadwick, also joined in. They did brave work at the Prague end, at considerable risk to themselves, because they had to deal on a daily basis with the head of the Gestapo there in negotiating and organizing the trains we needed. They also had a harrowing time interviewing desperate parents seeking priority.

All of these people who involved themselves as volunteers were normally employed in quite different professions. Nicholas Winton was a stockbroker, Trevor Chadwick was a schoolmaster, and Bill Barazetti, a longtime anti-Nazi, was working for the Czech secret service in Germany. Both he and Trevor Chadwick were daring and colorful characters who each escaped from some dangerous scrapes.

There were also several unsung voluntary heroines in Prague. For instance, Beatrice Wellington, a Canadian, and Josephine Pike, a convent-educated linguist and still a teenager, who looked after groups of children personally, struggled with the local Gestapo to ensure our escape, and accompanied many children to safety at the risk of their own lives. This must have been the same Miss Wellington whose office my mother often besieged. She worked at the Czech Refugee Institute in Prague, and when Doreen Warriner had to leave because her own life was in danger, Miss Wellington took over there, too, until she had seen the last 120 women and children from Sudetenland to safety. For although the Jewish children were being allowed out legally, the former Sudetenland refugees leaving via Poland were not. She was interrogated, standing, for six hours at a time, twice, and never divulged the full activities of her office. More of these details are constantly coming to light, and several more people than I've mentioned worked beyond the call of duty to help us.

We know now that the bureaucracy in Prague had become a shambles. There seemed to be five lists of children, and no one there knew how to get them sorted out. Bill Barazetti managed to meld the lists into one. Nicholas Winton got his mother to help, even placing advertisements in the newspapers in England asking for foster homes for those children still without guarantors, with pictures of appealing-looking children in the ads. The sorting of priorities was such a nightmare that I only now fully appreciate the incredible luck of my own escape; it may have helped, I think, that a home had already been arranged for me to go to. Things were desperate, and no one knew how much time was left.

The British Parliament had agreed, under pressure put by leading Jews on the Home Secretary, Samuel Hoare, to allow 10,000 unaccompanied Jewish children to enter the country, on condition that each was guaranteed by a host family and that various other strict conditions were met. Fares had to be paid by the guarantor, homes guaranteed until the age of eighteen, and the upper age limit on admission was seventeen. The Germans were at this stage still willing to allow as many as had entry visas to another country to leave, and the British supplied these 10,000, but as my mother's letters showed, the pressure put by families on those places was intense, and luck played quite a big part. Among these 10,000 places, only 669 Czech children escaped. The rest came from the other European countries where Jews were under threat. On September 3, 1939, one train filled with the biggest transport of all—250 Czech children—

was ready to leave Prague station. But because war broke out on that day, the Germans turned it back, and those children were murdered, as were most of the parents of those who had already escaped.

My mother had grasped one place and sent me on ahead. While writing this, I've wondered what she felt about the child whose chance for a permit we took. Or even what I feel about it. These were the trainloads of children that have only recently become known as the Kindertransport. When you come to think about it, it was with this name that we became a recognized group. It's too simple, really; name a group, and it's a recognized entity. But didn't this one take a long time to find?

The part played by these men and women has become widely known only since about 1989. Most had already died by then, but both Nicholas Winton and Bill Barazetti have been recognized for the part they played in saving our lives. Nicholas Winton has received many honors, including the Freedom of the City of Prague, and Bill Barazetti has been recognized by the State of Israel as a Righteous Gentile.

The whole thing came full circle for me while I was recording life stories for the National Sound Archive in London in the early nineties. I had the amazing chance to interview Nicholas Winton and hear about, and record, his life and work at that time. He is now over ninety, still very active, and in touch with many of the adult children he helped save.

Interviewing and being interviewed for these archives was in itself one of the early healing processes. It was the first time that a national organization concerned with recording *all* types of British lives had recognized and shown an interest in our stories. Not just our escape, but in our whole lives, and the effect that escape from persecution, loss of our parents, families, homes, country, language, school and religion, our entire background, had upon the rest of our lives, and our relationships with others and the world. We were now seen as a significant part of history.

It was also my first chance to commemorate my parents and make a contribution to the remembrance of all those who had died. It meant that I was able now to hear and record the lives of others, both Kindertransport and camp survivors. Sharing these experiences helped both sides. And some of my fellow interviewers recorded the hidden children, too. Getting together to discuss progress and share experiences, we too formed a group, and it all felt very real in a way that nothing quite had before. I suppose in this situation I had ceased to hide, but I also had a new pride in my right to exist and the pleasure of contributing in an honest way. Contributing is another essential part of healing. You cease to be the powerless recipient of charity.

Even more good things awaited us. One of the Kinder, Bertha Leverton, had felt as I did, but she did a great deal more about it. In 1988, when she realized that the fiftieth anniversary of her arrival in England was approaching and nothing was being done to commemorate it, she decided to do it herself. What she had envisaged as a small local get-together in London grew into a thousand-strong international reunion instead. She then founded the Reunion of Kindertransport, with its own newsletter, its search organization for lost friends and relations, and many other benefits. Soon after, the Holocaust Survivors Centre opened in London, and the Kindertransportees were included, albeit just a *tiny* bit reluctantly—we didn't *really* suffer enough, did we? It had dawned on me many years ago that there was a hierarchy of suffering, and we were at the bottom.

Altogether there was an absolute explosion of organizations, lectures, books, research, films, plays, both about us and about the Holocaust in general. Now we are fashionable! We even say, "There's no business like Shoah business!" But, not to be cynical, I am deeply grateful. It has somehow returned us to normality. We have a recognizable, widely acknowledged group; we are even, almost, respectable.

This business of needing a defined group is strange, but it must be an absolutely basic human need, for it to have been missed so badly when it was absent. I suppose, when you come to think about it, this is what nationalism is based on and, taken to extremes, causes all the trouble. Yet its total absence seems to be destructive to an individual's sense of self-worth.

Nowadays the British and international press mention Jews every day, quite normally. And it was at this recent time that my young friend, in her thirties, questioned me in all innocence about what could ever be wrong with us (see chapter 1). It was a mystery to her. She did not think we were dirty or deplorable. This was such a relief to me. It meant that the younger generation is not on the whole tainted with anti-Semitism. But I fear we know that other groups are scapegoated instead. And there are neo-Nazi groups already. So we do have to be vigilant.

I noticed also in 2001 that the BBC not only broadcast joint Jewish-Christian services at Easter but also taught the great British public the meaning of the Jewish festival of Pesach. I was ready to faint with amazement.

Reflecting seriously on the problems of recovery from loss, I and all the former refugees I know have found it to be a long, hard road. With no guidance, we had first to negotiate the minefield of grief. In our case, grief was not acknowledged as having an existence; in fact, it may have been seen as an insult to our host families, and therefore was in many cases hidden from ourselves and everyone around us. Even over a very long period of time. But such grief doesn't go away. Pushed underground, it came out as loneliness, depression, feelings of poor self-worth, and anger, which we were impotent to express. This no doubt varied very much according to each individual's experience. Some children were sent from homes that were already unhappy or broken. If they then had an unhappy foster experience, their suffering was extra severe. Others were truly lucky and were warmly welcomed into generous loving families who actually made them feel at home. There were many variables.

I also wonder, on further reflection, whether children are capable of allowing themselves the full experience and expression of grief at all. Maybe the sudden break with parents is so dislocating and the effects so profound that even if they are offered help, young children cannot handle and work through these emotions until they are older. And by that time, their feelings may be too buried to be easily excavated and worked through.

Among the former refugees I have talked with, the "not allowed" aspects of their loss and hidden grief were seen as an insuperable insult, an inhibition of their feelings, and therefore a huge handicap in recovery. It also provoked enormous anger, which sometimes erupted in misdirected ways.

Of course, in our particular case, the problem was so strung out in terms of time: first the parting, with hope of reunion; then the long period, years even, of separation and not knowing, coupled with whatever adaptation we were making; then finally the knowledge of loss, without outside recognition or empathy. It was really too complex for anyone to handle. By not having a specific time or place to grieve, and in many cases without knowledge of the place or circumstances of the deaths or respectful burial, the loss became open-ended. It was hard to bring it to a close; for many of us it took fifty years or more.

Among psychiatric workers in the field of grief work with children, some feel that early intervention to try to help is essential, while others feel that the immediate need of the bereaved child is a warm and sympathetic substitute for the lost parent. Psychiatric workers do hold the view that a child, while very young, is incapable of formulating and expressing feelings of grief verbally. But later, usually in adolescence, such feelings become more conscious, and it is at that point that help is needed and can be used. I believe, however, that ideally the warmth and the understanding would best go hand in hand at an early stage, to be gently verbalized by the adult to the child, even if the child cannot at that stage say very much. It is, I think, a matter about which we still need to learn.

In my own case, the experience of being made to feel a bad person and not belonging caused a lot of grief and conflict. Loneliness and unhappiness were ever present. I was not fully conscious at first that I had to grieve for my parents as well as recover from the effects of my subsequent upbringing. At first, the latter seemed like the primary problem. In a way it was. A happy experience would have made the loss far easier to bear.

However, having always wrestled with problems internally and read psychology books to help me solve them, I applied myself to reading. The trigger for my grief came from the first book I read about the camps, *Five Chimneys,* by Olga Langyel, which was published in 1947. I read this in 1950, when I was eighteen, and that was the first time I was able to cry. But the problem didn't go away. With adulthood and independence and standing on my own two feet, alone in the world, the loneliness increased.

Another alienating factor was that, having been forced to leave school at fifteen to earn a living, I was right out of my mind in a nurses' hostel. I decided to be as good a nurse as I could possibly be. I liked and was fascinated by the patients, and I loved medicine and didn't want to shortchange anyone, so I planned to get all my qualifications and get out. This took five years of what would now be regarded as hard labor. We worked twelve- to fourteen-hour heavy, hectic days, without support staff, modern shortcuts, or adequate labor laws. We were given huge responsibility for our age but treated like juvenile delinquents; the discipline was repressive and punitive. No normal emotions could be expressed, we had no support whatever, and our status felt nil. When the senior doctors entered the ward, we actually had to open the door for them and bow. We were chronically tired and spent our short free time sleeping, and, of course, our pay was tiny.

By now I was desperate to use my brain and ready to study. I read on my own, all the classics, Plato, Aristotle, Tolstoy, de Maupassant, politics and current events. As Elsie had foreseen, I didn't have the math or science to study medicine, and there were no evening catch-up classes then. I discovered that one college at London University, the London School of Economics, let people with deprived schooling in, on the basis of their experience and other qualifications, entrance exams, and interviews. God Bless the L.S.E.! They said they were looking for people who were able to think. I had arrived at intellectual and emotional paradise. No more subservience. It was possible to step back and look at the world dispassionately, to analyze it, not to feel helplessly enmeshed by it, and everyone was angelic to us. But I was still depressed with loneliness, which by now felt as if it might really be due to my own "badness."

I'd saved what money I could and won two small scholarships, and Doris's sister, Kathleen, who kept her eyes out for everyone, got one of her brothers to provide living accommodation. I paid my way a bit by answering his phones at night. Again, though, it was an abnormal home in that no one spent any time in it or ever exchanged any meaningful conversation. I was gruffly told the rules when I arrived: play ball, and you can stay—meaning, don't gossip with the servants or upset anyone. And I was very much not part of his family, but he was kind and generous, and, I'm sure, felt sorry for me.

Eventually I had enough training to work in the psychiatric field as a social worker, counselor, and teacher. I loved it and felt entirely at home. It didn't even feel like work. The therapeutic help I needed for myself was easily available, and I found it absolutely invaluable. But all my life, I've felt there was a doctor in there who never got out.

Among the former refugees I've met, this is an almost universal experience. We are underachievers in relation to our intelligence and talents. Most of us left school prematurely and had to earn a living at once. We carried emotional baggage that used up energy. In my own case, as well as being in a second-choice career, I consciously avoided leadership roles, fearful of provoking any more hostility.

Eventually, with marriage and children, things were much better, but the "adrift in the world" feeling, and not belonging anywhere, stayed. I was lucky to have access to an exceptional library of Holocaust literature. I read the stacks from end to end. I needed to. Maybe I even became addicted to reading them. I seemed to find that I needed to share my parents' experience in order to feel closer to them and to mourn the loss properly. It was a lot of suffering, but it felt right.

But the stage came when I really needed to let go of it all. This didn't happen until I met others with the same experience, but I didn't realize that this was what I needed. Even at that late stage, I didn't stop to think, Where are the other kids? Their existence still didn't cross my mind. Nor that I needed to meet them. Yet the knowledge must have been there, semiconscious, because I did realize that there was an absence of literature about experiences like mine, and this puzzled me. This was in the seventies and early eighties.

I therefore did not realize until about 1989 what a variety of problems we had all met. For instance, that many children lacked private homes to go to and went straight into hostels organized by the Refugee Children's Movement, which had been hastily formed in 1939 to deal with this urgent child-refugee problem. This movement then provided the guarantees necessary for admitting the children to Britain without private guarantors. And even when homes were found after the children entered the hostels, it was a rushed and chancy business. Until the first Kindertransport reunion, I had not even known that these hostels existed, had not realized just how many children were placed there and what painful experiences they too went through. Many were not lucky when foster homes were offered. Many were rejected for arbitrary reasons and remained in the institutional environment and never experienced a home life again. Some of the older ones were fostered but were used as servants immediately. Each of us seemed to go through a varying sequence of events. Each of us had different problems and dealt with them differently. But when we eventually got together to share them, we found there were some remarkable and comforting similarities in experience and reaction.

Listening to one another was and still is so helpful. I learn more every time. Just the existence of a group that shares and understands such feelings is comforting and healing. My own experiences, acknowledged as unhappy, fall into place beside those that were as bad or worse. We can see an increase of happiness in individuals. Vera Schaufeld and I now exchange birthday cards each year. We each know what we feel about birthdays.

We do all seem to need a group, a sense of belonging. Ours had been taken away. It's taken us fifty to sixty years to find one again. It seems that no amount of therapy, or real-life good experiences, can quite do what sharing a joint trouble with one similarly afflicted can do. This has long been known in the medical field. There are groups for every kind of ailment or suffering, but ours took very many years to come about because it took a long time for us to realize that we needed it.

I've noticed an interesting development in relation to my adoptive family when we've gathered several times in the last ten years at parties or funerals. It is quite a big family, as Doris was one of six, and all her siblings had several children, too. They are all long-lived, and there are many cousins. For years I felt like a pathetic outsider. But after making a family of my own and sorting out my problems, I felt confident and cheerful and met them as equals. Not only were they charming to me, but I realized that in a strange way I fulfilled a tiny function in this family. Being just a little bit outside it, and of a sort of median age between all of them, I suddenly saw that I met some small need.

They were genuinely pleased to see me and were no doubt relieved that I didn't look pathetic or defensive. One by one, they came to talk and confided some family news that I had known nothing about. I was sufficiently trusted and yet outside the family enough to be safe to talk to. I was amused and touched. And this could only come about because a benign circle had developed. Confidence breeds ease and respect, and good things follow.

As far as my own recovery is concerned, I am convinced that heredity and luck played a very big part. I have my mother's determination and strength. I had an unusual role model in her. I'd also had six and a half good years with both parents. I had a tremendous interest in mental health and the determination to work at achieving my own. All these things came together to help me achieve it. But it was constant hard work, and there were long periods when things didn't look so good, and many people didn't have those advantages. Above all, no child should have been put in the position we were in, and many have not been so lucky as to be able to recover.

8
Full Circle

Immediately after Central and Eastern Europe opened up, following their sudden freedom from Communist rule in 1989, it seemed a good idea to visit Prague. It would be my first visit there since 1947, when I was only fifteen. I had never been back to my own home, or seen the area where I lived with my parents, since I left in 1939. It had been under either Nazi or Communist rule almost the whole of that time except for a short period just after the end of the war. I decided that going in an ordinary, non-Jewish organized group would minimize the trauma. My husband came with me. I had been very fearful of getting caught there all the years the Communists were in power. The words "Born in Prague" were on my passport. I felt that I'd escaped from the Nazis, but then the Communists took over very soon after my postwar visit. My fear may have been irrational, but I'd kept away for a long time and did not feel too comfortable even now. In 1989, all the good things I've described had happened. I prepared by getting the address of the home I'd left, from my mother's letters, and studying the map of Prague. I also got my cousin Jana, Aunt Zdena's daughter, to write me a note in Czech, as I wanted to see if I could ask to enter the flat, my old home.

We went first to Budapest and Vienna, neither of which I'd seen before, and finished up in Prague. It really was only a month or two since it had opened up. Everyone was new to freedom, but freedom hadn't brought better conditions. I believe that initially people became poorer through inflation, and some still are now, although others have since prospered. At any rate, they had been oppressed for as long as they could remember. The city, apart from the central preserved areas of history and beauty, was gray and drab. Shop windows almost empty. When goods did come in, people queued up and stocked up in case such things did not return.

Above all the people themselves looked drab, depressed and sullen. They must have resented Western visitors in many ways. The food in the hotels was inexpensive and good. I don't know if anyone was being deprived while we were being fed.

After settling in, we opened up the map and spread it out on the bed. We had been allocated this hotel by the travel company. We had no idea where it would be. I had noticed that the street sign on the corner as our bus came toward the hotel said "Prague 7," but thought no more of it. We looked on the map and found that the hotel was on the main street facing a side road, and on the map we could see that it was my old road, Šimáčkova. And we could see not only what was probably my old apartment block but probably the flat itself from the window. Out into the street, across the road, and we were there, 22 Šimáčkova.

I clutched my cousin's letter in my hand, realizing that I couldn't remember which floor the flat was on. I did have a clear picture of being able, as a child, to see across the landing and down the stairs, and this helped us locate the correct side of the building. We tried the first floor but got no answer. On the next, a woman answered and, on being shown the note, smiled nicely and let us in.

The flat was exactly as I remembered it, except that there was a nasty-looking dark carpet covering the parquet. The rooms with the connecting doors were there, and above all, the view toward the main road where I had seen the German soldiers marching in when they invaded. Later, in the evening, I asked the guide, who was Czech, "Where did the Germans enter Prague?" She said, "From west to east, along the main road over there." Of course, it is possible that I got the level of the apartment wrong. I expect they all had the same layout, at least on that side, but since I remember looking down on the soldiers' helmets, it was probably right. The flat did have one room more than I remembered, a small bedroom. I realized afterward that it must have been the room for the nanny.

We walked around the neighborhood. Round the corner was a kindergarten. That must have been the one, it was very near. Then the park. Just for old time's sake, I sat on all the swings. We photographed the house, including the tiny yard filled with garbage cans. From the park I took a yellowish stone as a souvenir.

We visited the Jewish quarter, of course, and the Prague Jewish Museum, where I asked for details of my relatives. I was very lucky to be one of the first visitors, for they sent me a list of the deportations of my family within a week or two. Only my grandfather were they unable to trace, because I had forgotten the information in Heda's letter about his death in Oranienberg, and had misinformed the museum about him, thinking his first name was Josef and that he had actually been shot outright in the street.

By the time my friend Vera Schaufeld tried for the same information a few months later, the museum had presumably been inundated with queries and didn't reply. I walked around, and asked myself if I felt at home. I did feel I had the right to be there. But I felt angry that the Czech government hadn't been able to protect its children.

The most beneficial feeling was knowing that I hadn't imagined it all. I had kept that apartment in my mind for fifty years, and it really was there, exactly as I remembered. It really had all happened, I hadn't imagined it. I had drawn a diagram of the flat for my husband in advance, so we knew I wasn't fantasizing.

I tried also to find the cobbler's shop, the one who put the jewelry in the heels of my boots, but failed. We also couldn't find Grannie's, or what should now be my, house, at Hloubětín. The no. 5 tram left from the bus stop at the end of my road, outside the hotel. I could hardly believe that this must have been the stop from which we traveled to see Grannie every Sunday. It definitely must have been. And as the trams looked so ancient, I should think they could have been the same ones.

I'd hoped to see my family's names engraved on the walls of the Pinkas Synagogue, which commemorates all the Czechs who died, but it was closed for repairs.

A few months later, in the summer of the next year, our elder daughter and I made another trip, this time around all of Czechoslovakia, including Prague. I showed her the outside of the apartment, and one evening, very late, for it was dark on a July night, we were traveling on the bus into Prague again and passed the station, which was huge, cavernous and brightly lit, the one from which I'd left fifty-one years ago. I wish I could say that this was also July 18, but I can only say that it was very close to that date!

To know the whereabouts and to visit the place where our loved ones have either died or been buried seems to be another basic human need, and one that had been denied all those of us whose parents perished we knew not where. I was one of the "lucky" ones who did know where my parents had died, even to the exact spot as described by my cousins, who were witnesses. I had always resented there having been no funeral, no acknowledgment of them, or even a memorial of any kind.

After this great opening up of information, once survivors and Kindertransportees became recognized entities even among Jews who had formerly turned away their eyes, the memorial aspects were put right. Various memorial services were held at Jewish places of worship or study, and I attended a couple of these and found it helpful. I felt they were belated marks of respect for people who had been virtually ignored. How dared anyone feel that we should forget about them, or that they were unworthy of being remembered?

At the Sternberg Centre in London, the center for the study of Judaism, there is a memorial garden, and I was happy to attend a ceremony there. Even better, the now well-known Smith family, as Christians, felt such a sense of shame at what the Christians had done to the Jews that they set up Beth Shalom, a teaching and memorial center in the countryside near Nottingham, to teach the history of this period to schoolchildren, students, and visitors from around Britain and the world, to try to increase knowledge and understanding and give recognition to the victims and their descendants. All of us who are connected to these events are given a warm welcome there. There is a white rose garden at Beth Shalom, for any of us who wish to have a rose planted in memory of loved ones. And, of course, I sent my family's names to Yad Vashem in Jerusalem, to be commemorated there forever.

But, except for the memorial facility at Yad Vashem, all the commemorative activity in England has come about chiefly in the last thirteen years. At Yad Vashem, when I went in 1990, to check whether our family names were there, the welcome surprised us. The desk was manned by volunteers. On the day that my husband and I went, we waited behind an American woman who was making an inquiry on behalf of the Holocaust Center in Pittsburgh, where she worked as a volunteer. She seemed to irritate our Israeli charmer, for he responded, "Pittsburgh, Schmittsburg, I don't care where you come from, this is Jerusalem." However, in spite of him, I feel very satisfied that proper respect has now been paid in a lot of quarters.

While being deeply appreciative of these acknowledgments and all the work, generosity, and abounding goodwill they represent, I think we must be watchful that a wholesale "love of Jews" does not become as categorizing and eventually as separating as anti-Semitism itself. But there's hardly a risk of that happening on a large scale!

So there was one more visit that needed to be made.

I'd spent years reading the Holocaust literature. Scores and scores of books, even hundreds. In each one I met new horrors I'd never dreamed of. It was not just a wish to get closer to my parents but also a duty, to know what all these people had gone through. I read picture journals as well as many, many memoirs. One picture from Auschwitz particularly stays in my mind. It shows a long line of doctors, who were kept till the last, all waiting to be gassed together. Think about those six million killed and about what Jews have already contributed to the world. Whatever more has been lost? Think of those one and a half million children. The trouble is, it doesn't bear thinking about. Worse still, many Germans have never bothered, or been obliged, to think about it at all.

So after all this reading and grieving, I felt that Auschwitz was only too clearly imprinted on my mind. I had in some ways identified with the suffering so much that I felt I'd at least shared some of it mentally. I wanted to share that suffering with my parents. Not that they would have demanded it, but I needed to feel it myself. I did not want to distance myself from it and, above all, from them.

There was no question of visiting while Poland was under Communist rule, and for a long time I had never imagined doing so; and in any case while I was still so full of grief and even fear and horror, engendered by what I had read, I could not have done it. But when Eastern Europe opened up, it became possible.

For some years I couldn't face it. I felt oppressed by the barbed wire myself, the watchtowers, the railway lines bringing the cattle trucks filled with people into the camp. The gray terror of it gripped me. I had so identified with the suffering that I formed a picture in my mind, of myself on the ground, looking at the earth, like the people I first read about years ago, dirty, cold, starving, and despairing. I heard that parties of Jewish mourners were making pilgrimages; I couldn't face that either.

But then I heard about a Jewish travel agent who was organizing day trips. I didn't want to stay long(!), so maybe I could manage this. A day trip to such a place may sound obscene, almost disrespectful, but I don't really think so. Do we owe the torturers longer? It certainly wouldn't help the dead. And my respect isn't in any doubt.

In order to face it at all, I found I had to distance myself just a tiny bit, just for that day. I chose to go alone so I could concentrate. I did not want to look after anyone else who might become upset. I had already done my homework and was pretty sure I could cope. No place for such thoughts, anyway. Our families didn't have such a choice, did they? My family was very supportive; all our children wanted to hear about it, and my husband stayed at home, thinking about it and shedding tears. So I felt very lucky to be in such a good supported state for such a visit.

There was a planeload of 220 Jews of every persuasion. I am such an ignorant Jew, religiously, that I had to ask Vera afterwards what a snood worn on the head meant. It seems it denotes one level less of orthodoxy than a wig.

I've lived among Christians for the major part of my life and feel more alien among practicing Jews than among foreigners of any kind. Perhaps what feels so unpleasant is the discomfort of realizing that I have lost the sense of familiarity that should belong to me by right, and that I really am an outsider in every society, including what should be my own.

Yet, another Jewish friend says she *likes* being an outsider everywhere, that it's more interesting and gives her freedom. Now, after so much healing, I can to some extent share that view. And yet. . . .

They all wore black and I didn't. There's a form of belonging in each different section of Jewry. My own group is that of those vestigial Jews who were robbed of their whole Jewishness and who share their outsiderness with others of their kind. Just as I find there exist groups of what I call professional Christians, who are not necessarily ordained in the church, I find the same among Jews. I'm sure this applies to every religion.

I would have loved to talk to all of them, ask them why they wanted to visit. Most seemed far more peripherally involved than I was. Some even gave the impression that it had become the fashionable thing to do. Almost something to go back to the synagogue to boast about. That you needed your Holocaust colors, however distant, even nonexistent, to make your connection with what has become the communal, mythologized, suffering. Perhaps it was in expiation of never having suffered at all. I didn't like to think about the loud exclamations of horror and admiration when they told their friends in the congregation about their visit. But I shouldn't take a crabbed attitude. Everyone should go, and reflect about human nature. I am sure, in fact, that they were sincere in their hearts.

But many in the group had their own quiet reasons for being there. One man told me he had come to explore his Jewishness. Another, sitting next to me on the bus, exclaimed as we approached, still a little distance from Auschwitz, when he saw a single railway line, "There is the line!" It struck me hard, that we had all come with our fantasies, to confirm or refute them.

The first thing to be seen when the bus drew up in the Auschwitz compound was a kiosk selling film. The next was a sign sticking out from the wall inside the building, saying HOT DOGS. Our guide lived nearby and was half Jewish and half Polish Catholic. He had survived the war as a young boy by doing slave labor in a local factory. I recognized everything from all the books and my cousin's accounts, but it was sanitized, spotlessly clean. And, contrary to some reports, the birds were singing, the grass was growing. As I walked between the rows of immaculate barracks beside a man I didn't know, he said, "There's no atmosphere of evil. You can't believe it all happened here."

We were taken into the basement, past tiny interrogation rooms, starvation rooms, the SS men's off-duty room. I don't know what I expected. Did I really think the blood would still be there? The prisoner's striped uniform was clean and ironed, hanging on the back of a chair. The rows of open latrines were also spotless. I felt a little worried, I think, that anyone seeing all this who hadn't read the books would really have no idea how bad it had been. But how else could it be displayed? Many schoolchildren come each year. There were eleven busloads of visitors the day in April when I was there.

We were taken by bus to the Birkenau section of Auschwitz, where the Czech camp and my parents had been. Those of us who wanted to climbed to the top of the watchtower. There was an engraved bronze map of the entire compound, so I was able to see the exact spot, which my cousin described, close to the birch trees at the edge, where all the Czechs had been killed.

We then walked up the railway line along which my parents and all the others had been brought. At the top of the field was Mengele's so-called clinic, half fallen down and looking like a sculpture with all the uprights meeting at the top center from an angle, a bit like a broken fossilized tent, with gaps between the struts. The gas chamber and crematoria were right beside it, still there.

I then heard the guide say words I had never expected to hear. He said, "Ladies and gentlemen, will you follow me into the gas chamber?" And we did. He showed us where the fires had been lit and the ashes shoveled out. He expounded on the strength and power of the cylinders that had created the heat. He told us that above one of the larger crematoria the Germans had their café and sick bay. We also saw the commandant's house, hard by the outer wall of the camp. Wife and children had lived there, too.

Just outside the crematoria were some stagnant shallow puddles over which flies were hovering. The guide told us that the fine, yellowish gray earth we saw was human ash several feet deep. This ash had apparently also been used to scatter (presumably as fertilizer!) on surrounding fields and to rebuild Polish houses.

Near this area of murder is now a memorial spot, a sort of amphitheater with rows of ascending steps. The rabbi who accompanied us said a Kaddish for the dead and read out the names of family members who had been killed there; some people left lighted candles in memory.

Of course we were also taken to the museum, where some of the horrors are displayed. The huge display case of Jewish hair, all gray from the gas, and a piece of cloth the Germans had woven from this hair. Another of empty canisters of the poison gas Zyklon-B. Another huge area of artifacts the prisoners had brought into the camp with them, confiscated at once but not so valuable as to be sent immediately to Germany. Thousands of utensils, mostly enamel. Buckets, bowls, jugs. I could even recognize national designs painted on them. These gripped me; I thought of the lives that had been attached to each of these homely things. Yet another room was filled with suitcases with the labels still attached and the names and addresses still visible. Of course all this filled us all with impotent rage.

There was another memorial area in a dimly lit underground room, where another short service was held. Several of the women were properly equipped with candles. I was too ignorant to have brought any; our branch of the Christian church is a candle-free zone, and anyway I am not fond of conventional sentimental gestures. But one of the women gave me a candle to light and leave there. She knew I had come to mark my parents, and I felt touched by her care.

The guide told us that 50,000 Germans visit each year. Over a ten-year period that is only half a million. Should it not be compulsory?

I was very glad I had been. It was a duty I had wanted to fulfill and another mark of contact and respect that I needed to make.

Eighteen months later, a follow-up meeting was held in London. It was called "So You've Been to Auschwitz. Where To Now?"

All 3,000 people who had taken part in the day trips were invited, and several hundred came. The meeting was organized by the rabbi Barry Marcus, who had led us, in conjunction with the Holocaust Educational Trust. He had, we learned, been the inspiration behind the day trips because he wanted not only Jews but also Christians to see for themselves what had happened. He likes to take Christian religious teachers and senior schoolchildren and students, whenever such a group can be arranged.

There were four rabbis present at this meeting. All spoke in impassioned terms, and the gist of their message was that after Auschwitz, we must lead lives more in keeping with the Ten Commandments of Moses and marry within the religion. And (unspoken) that we should have a lot of Jewish children, educating them and bringing them up in the Jewish way. We were told that Jewish schools had recently been set up in Hungary to do just this. If we did not, we would be perpetuating Hitler's achievement in almost destroying the Jews. This, it seems, is happening already, as more and more young Jews are marrying out.

At the same time, the rabbis deplored the division between Christians and Jews, and one lone Christian present asked, "Why *is* it 'you' and 'us'?" The rabbis' speeches were not well received by the audience, who had clearly not come for a religious sermon, least of all an Orthodox one, and a Jewish quarrel threatened to break out, which was rapidly halted by the rabbis. Several camp survivors also spoke, and they did not take kindly to the religious sermons either. They had been practicing religious Jews before they were tortured, and had God looked after them then?

Their protests echoed my own uneasy thoughts. Surely the more we accentuate the differences between all humans by practicing and perpetuating our own brand of religion and life, the more divided the world will be? So that, like all the religious wars past and present, far from bringing us together, it divides us further. Could the lesson of the Holocaust be that we should *not* be different? Perhaps *all* races and religions should intermingle? This is a heretical thought that could get me stoned, but I think it is in the unconscious or conscious minds of those who are choosing to intermingle and lessen group differences themselves.

No doubt the true believers would tell me that I am merely perpetuating my own brainwashing regarding the "unacceptability" of us Jews and the "acceptability" of Christians. And they, too, could be right. Since I have no religious Jewish background, I was certainly susceptible to all other religious and social influences.

I could have made my own protest to these rabbis if I'd wished, about the shortage of Jewish homes with open doors in 1939, when we children needed them most. And where were the rabbis who should have made sure that the doors of their congregations were open? They are actually blaming us *now* for being insufficiently Jewish?

As this problem of identity is not merely theoretically perplexing but threatens the peace of the world, I cannot accept the notion that togetherness can be brought about by increasing our numbers and perpetuating our differences. Ideally, I suppose, the rabbis are preaching increased numbers *and* tolerance. But neither Jews, Catholics, Protestants, nor Muslims and the rest have managed this feat of tolerance so far.

My attitude can be understood in context. I was propelled outside all belief systems that could possibly "belong" to me. I've had to start from scratch, as have all of us refugees, and perhaps that's led to a paradoxically good outcome, even if it has caused us extreme discomfort all our lives. Perhaps it's good to think all this through, independent of emotional identification. We have a degree of objectivity that insiders cannot have. If only that were enough to find a solution.

Postscript

In July 1999, at a family party in London for Aunt Zdena's eighty-fifth birthday, Helena Milek-Grant, a Czech survivor cousin-in-law from Switzerland, gave me an article she had found in the Prague Jewish Library. It was from the Jewish Yearbook of 1997 and was part of an article by Frantisek Fuchs, "The Anti-Nazi Struggle of the Czech Jews in Terezin."

My aunt translated the article for me, and after I'd read it, I knew I could no longer postpone writing this book.

I quote the following passage from it:

> The old socialist and Trade Union worker Viteslav Stein [my grandfather] provided regular news bulletins to Yugoslavia until he was arrested on the 28th October 1939. He died soon after that in the concentration camp in Oranienburg.
>
> His daughter Anna Rothová also deserves to be remembered. The way she fought the pressures put upon the Jews by the Gestapo is a magnificent example of an everyday heroism; she carried out mundane, routine work in the name of humanism in the worst of conditions.
>
> When the Germans forbade all manner of teaching for the Jewish children, she organised under the name of 'shelters', secret schooling for them, in the Jewish Town Hall.
>
> In the shelters, it was permitted to 'keep the children busy', so they shouldn't roam idly in the streets. The shelters of Anna Rothová became

gradually an exemplary experimental school where children got educated in a democratic spirit and with a firm purpose in mind.

Rothová kept working in the same vein in Terezin and, with a fanatic determination, even in Auschwitz, where she perished in 1944 in the gas chamber

BIBLIOGRAPHY

REFERENCE VOLUMES

Carter, George. *Outlines of English History.* West Sussex, England: Ward Lock Educational Company, 1962.

Chronology of British History. Brockhampton Reference Series. London: Hodder Headline, 1995.

World History. Brockhampton Reference Series. London: Hodder Headline, 1995.

PERIODICALS, HANDBOOKS, AND REPORTS

Beth Shalom Handbook. Nottingham, England: Holocaust Centre, Beth Shalom.

Holocaust Memorial Day, Winter 2000 (special issue). *Perspectives: A Journal of the Holocaust Memorial Centre.* Nottingham, England: Holocaust Centre, Beth Shalom.

Kohn, Paul. "The Rescued Children." *Holocaust Educational Trust Annual Report, 1998–99.* London: Holocaust Educational Trust, 2000. (Reprinted from the *Jerusalem Post,* Dec. 1, 1988.)

Pearson, Sue. "Henry Fair." In the handbook of the Kindertransport 60th Anniversary, 1999. London: Institute of Contemporary History and Wiener Library (archive).

Posner, Susan, and Gissing, Vera. "Winton's Wartime Gesture." In the handbook of the Kindertransport 60th Anniversary, 1999. London: Institute of Contemporary History and Wiener Library (archive).

Presland, John. "A Great Adventure: The Story of the Refugee Children's Movement." In the handbook of the Kindertransport 60th Anniversary, 1999.

London: Institute of Contemporary History and Wiener Library (archive). (Originally published July 1944.)

"Rabbi Dr. Solomon Schonfeld: A Commemoration" (obituary). In the handbook of the Kindertransport 60th Anniversary, 1999. London: Institute of Contemporary History and Wiener Library (archive). (Originally published July 1944.)

Remembering for the Future, 2000: The Holocaust in an Age of Genocide (conference handbook). London: Institute of Contemporary History and Wiener Library (archive).

"Timeline" (calendar of events, Jan. 1933–May 1945). In the handbook of the Kindertransport 60th Anniversary, 1999. London: Institute of Contemporary History and Wiener Library (archive). (Originally published July 1944.)

MEMOIRS AND STUDIES

Emanuel, Muriel, and Gissing, Vera. *Nicholas Winton and the Rescued Generation.* London: Vallentine Mitchell, 2002.

Girshon, Karen. *We Came As Children.* London: Victor Gollanz, 1966.

Leverton, Bertha, and Lowensohn, Shmuel. *I Came Alone.* Lewes, Sussex, England: The Book Guild, 1990.

Marks, Jane. *The Hidden Children.* London: Judy Piatcus, 1995.

Mendelsson, Steven, Schaufeld, Vera, and Vincent, Lisa, with Smith, Steven D. *Our Lonely Journey: Remembering the Kindertransports.* Laxton, Newark, Nottingham, England: Beth Shalom/Paintbrush Publications, 1999.

Segal, Lore Grozsman. *Other People's Houses.* New York: Harcourt, Brace & World, 1964.

Turner, Barry. *And the Policeman Smiled.* London: Bloomsbury Publishing, 1990.

Whiteman, Dorit Bader. *The Uprooted: A Hitler Legacy.* New York: Plenum Press, 1993.

INDEX